There is no excuse for ugliness

This is an abbreviation of a quotation ...

"THERE WAS NO EXCUSE FOR UGLINESS AS BEAUTY PROPERLY UNDERSTOOD WAS CHEAP"

... by Heronswood's architect EDWARD LA TROBE BATEMAN in a letter to Georgiana McCrae, a friend who lived nearby in what we now know as McCrae Homestead.

Fresh from working with Joseph Paxton in 1851 on the Crystal Palace, La Trobe arrived in Australia in search of gold in 1852. He was not your average digger – for when his luck ran out he found work designing homesteads such as Heronswood, Barragunda and Kolor, all of which are today listed on the Register of National Estate.

He also drew up designs for Carlton, Fitzroy and Ripponlea gardens and became a highly respected flower painter and illuminator before he left Australia in 1869.

"Bateman was the most talented and perhaps the most prolific Anglo-Australian landscape gardener of the 19th century." Bill Bampton

Thanks are due.

Just as I started to write this book the 'Eucalyptic' destroyed our office and about 25,000 slides collected over 30 years. It also destroyed about 12 months of digital files but thanks to an incredible effort by our publishing staff, particularly Caroline Trevorrow and Gordon Clarke, we managed to meet deadlines for our magazines as well as this book. I am indebted to Bill Bampton for his Basic Botany guide, Jeremy Francis for his words on Cloudehill and Tim Sansom and Marcus Ryan for assisting with the hugely complex Plant Selector, which involves about 8,000 codes to describe our selections.

Claire Takacs, a photographer of great renown, arrived miraculously the day before the fire and took enough pictures to more than make up for our loss. The fire had a huge impact on all our staff but Lisa Remato, Tim Sansom, Nikki Fraser, Talei Kenyon and my wife Penny's determination helped to re-energise us all.

Some of our visitors to Heronswood believe that I created the garden on my own working full time. The truth is I spent 5 days a week doing Diggers Club work at a desk and about 1½ days each week physically gardening until a not-to-be-named head gardener asked that I refrain! I always thought that the Cook and the Gardener was the most difficult gardening partnership but reconciling two gardening opinions can be trying too!

Of course, being the garden owner I'm the one left standing when our gardeners move on so I think I can claim some credit for its evolution and creation not to mention the pleasure in working with every one of our gardeners. We owe an enormous debt to Dave Pomarre and to lots of other gardeners; Andrew Carpenter, Simon Rickard and latterly Priscilla van den Broek and Bill Bampton, Robyn Cole and Bernadette Brady.

Many visitors to Heronswood are intimidated by the thought of how much work it is to keep our garden at such a high standard but let me assure you that when we equate our 3 gardeners' hours from 3 acres to a 1/6 acre block it is about 5 hours gardening each week.

To be able to grow all your own food and to be surrounded by such garden beauty is surely worthwhile, not to mention that gardeners invariably enjoy longer and healthier lives than others.

First published in Australia, 2014
Reprinted September 2015

The Diggers Club
PO Box 300, Dromana, VIC Australia
Phone: 03 5984 7900
www.diggers.com.au

© Clive Blazey

Self-published Diggers titles:

The Australian Fruit and Vegetable Garden, Clive Blazey and Jane Varkulevicius, 2006
Growing Your Own Heirloom Vegetables, Clive Blazey, 2008
All About Tomatoes, Clive Blazey, 2011
There Is No Excuse For Ugliness, Clive Blazey, 2014

Other Diggers titles:

Guide to Gardening Success, 1994 (Transworld)
The Australian Vegetable Garden, Clive Blazey, 1999 (New Holland)
The Australian Flower Garden, 2001 (Penguin)
The Australian Vegetable Garden, Clive Blazey, 2012 (2nd edition, New Holland)

Front cover: Heronswood's summer border, 2014 by Claire Takacs.
A big thank you to Claire Takacs whose photography is featured throughout the book. Thanks also to Yanni for his photos of the Heronswood fire (p12, 128), Jaime Plaza, Royal Botanic Gardens and Domain Trust (p47) and Jellitto Staudensamen Gmbh for some images in the Plant Selector. All other images supplied by Diggers. Apologies if we've missed anyone – get in touch with us so we can amend it for the next issue.

Printed in China through Asia Pacific Offset Ltd.
Distributed by NewSouth Books.
UNSW Press, University of New South Wales
Sydney   NSW   2052   Phone: 02 8936 0100   Fax: 02 8936 0040

National Library of Australia Cataloguing-in-Publication entry.
Author: Blazey, Clive
Title: There is no excuse for ugliness - falling in love with the best plants and gardens.
ISBN: 978-0-646-91978-2
Notes: Includes index.
Subjects: Gardening and horticulture; heirloom flowers.
Dewey Number: 635

| 1994 | 1999 | 2001 | 2006 |
| 2008 | 2011 | 2012 | 2014 |

CONTENTS

We've been planting the wrong plants and gardens

▲ Penny and Clive Blazey at Heronswood in 1985.

There is hardly a country town on this vast continent with a successful, unbroken line of uniform street trees.

Whilst Australians have been fortunate to have been nurtured in an English gardening tradition we have little to show for it in contrast to our English forebears who, during this time, have been creating the finest gardens the world has seen. It is an unpalatable fact that during our 230 years of settlement we have created very few of our own gardens of international stature.

For too many years we have been planting the bush in suburbia or the picture book English garden in a hostile climate. In short, the wrong plants and gardens for permanence.

I've now been gardening for over 40 years creating the garden at Heronswood; supervising the Garden at St Erth and travelling to gardens in Italy, England, France, Holland, Germany and America.

Whilst studying at Melbourne University I made my first visit to Melbourne's Royal Botanic Gardens and was captivated by its beauty. Having been brought up surrounded by suburban gardens I decided there and then that this was the sort of garden I wanted to live in.

However it took quite a few years into a career in economics and marketing before I realised that a corporate life was not for me. I was too impatient to start another degree so a self-taught gardener I became.

To cope with my knowledge deficit I spent hours every night reading about plants and gardens and travelling overseas at every holiday time, determined to build my garden knowledge as quickly as possible.

At our home we set about growing our own flowers and food inspired by the TV programme *The Good Life*. We had a sheep to mow the lawn, Leunig ducks on the pond and a solar hot water system to cut our energy use. We started The Diggers Club in 1978 in a garage in Albert Park after Penny and I acquired a vacant, disused site from the nearby Convent of the Good Shepherd.

It would be another 21 years before I felt confident enough to write my first garden book outlining all the pitfalls beginners make when they garden as I did, learning from my own mistakes. It is now a further 20 years since this book was published and the standard of gardening has hardly improved.

We were brought up on Bob Dylan, The Beatles, Germaine Greer, David Suzuki and Bill Mollison's permaculture but whilst our generation rebelled against the Vietnam War, and ushered in the woman's movement and sustainable lifestyles, *the continuing horror of Australia's suburban gardening style became even more irritating.*

So that's what this book is designed to do.

To help you express your individuality by creating a beautiful garden that's anything but commonplace!

I would suggest that the getting of garden wisdom revolves around choosing between good and poor plants, which for most means judging a plant by its foliage and form and not being seduced by drop dead gorgeous flowers.

That long lasting pleasure that we all enjoy when we create a beautiful garden picture is all about colour harmonies and subtlety rather than when the eye is drenched with colour. *Less is more when we work with colour.*

▲ Typical suburban planting – bedding plants and roses.

Most gardens in Australia are flat and uninteresting in summer, not because we don't have enough heat and drought tolerant plants to choose from but simply because suburban gardeners continually, but inadvertently, select spring flowering plants in the forlorn hope that flowering will continue for months on end.

As you read this book I will show you that the humble vegetable garden, skilfully arranged, can be just as appealing as the most beautiful flower border. That there are many fruit trees that are handsome enough to fit in a beautiful garden. Shouldn't ornamental plants be edible as well?

I will also explain that our native eucalypt is about the worst choice of tree for summer shade, and that we should be planting our evergreen native rainforest trees instead.

Eucalyptus leaves hang down, providing little shade and letting heat through to the soil. ▲

If this all sounds too heretical then we must accept that gardening success in Australia does pose quite a challenge because we do have a harsher climate than almost any other country and the new Australian garden must take this into account. The very formal Italian garden style which influenced the creation of the garden at Versailles was supported by delusions of grandeur and obscene wealth; hardly applicable to our sense of place. The English landscape style does not translate into suburban sized blocks and 90% of plants that appear in English coffee table books that gardeners still consult for advice fail under our hot Australian sun. So an understanding of the climate range a plant will grow in is a vital threshold between success and failure. This has helped The Diggers Club establish heat and cold zone guides which are light years ahead of any climate tool in use in Australia today so be sure to use them.

▲ Colour overloads – typical suburban colour clashes.   LEFT Hybrid tea rose stems and leaves are ugly. ▼
RIGHT Werribee Park – too many roses!

Australia's botanic gardens are the most overlooked source of inspiration. I would go to Melbourne's botanic gardens every weekend with my wife and children to have breakfast and walk around taking notes, learning the names of plants I liked and inspiring my children with its incredible beauty. If this sounds a little bewildering don't give up. There is as much pleasure in the journey as there is in reaching the destination.

So start by creating a pleasing garden picture, which is the first step towards falling in love with your garden. *Gardening is a progression beyond the innocent cultivation of obvious plants.*

The Australian ugliness

▲ Too frequently part of visual suburbia; the complete absence of permanence – no trees, shrubs or perennials.

Robin Boyd's shock title *The Australian Ugliness* became a best seller in 1960 and began a debate that has traction even today.

Boyd's critique of the stylistic cowardice of the suburbs was a wake up call to Australian mediocrity, where architecture (and gardening) in the pursuit of respectability created a superficial sense of place.

"Hobart might have been beautiful if it hadn't chosen to be pretty" is a typical quote emphasising our pursuit of decorative kitsch.

If we go back 50-60 years as the postwar economic boom created new suburbs on the edges of our cities in Australia, almost every artistic field had a dynamism except the art of gardening.

We have buried our English culinary inheritance of meat and two veg and become one of the most vibrant food destinations in the world. In the visual arts of painting, film making and architecture Australian artists are thriving. Indeed our galleries, museums and concerts today are as well attended as our football stadiums.

The graduation of two generations of tertiary trained architects set much higher building standards in the succeeding years since the publication of Boyd's book; but suburbia is largely built by tradesmen builders.

Unfortunately for our gardens there has not been aesthetic uplift; in fact it is easier to argue there has been a decline. The commonplace garden continues on.

Why is bad taste so ubiquitous?

Our tradesmen driven nursery industry that supplies our plants is barely aware of how bad the suburban garden was and still is. In pursuing impulse driven annuals such as bedding plants and potted colour they put an even greater focus on decoration and impermanence than before.

Despite the recent ability of home owners to be able to afford advice, they are gullibly led by mass media TV programs into believing that gardens can be created instantly out of paving and flax, in short "survival rather than desirable gardens". Bereft of trees, the absence of shade raises temperatures, ensuring backyards are too hot to be enjoyed during summer.

Before the war every garden had fruit trees and a vegetable garden. But even then, within our botanic gardens and in our public spaces, edible plants were effectively banned. The creation of beauty in the production of food was never attempted.

Finally the transformation of the garden industry in the last 10 years by the big box warehouses (established in the ugliest of buildings) has been a calamitous step. It's the hardware driven approach to outdoor art that destroys all sensibility. Instead of relying on the traditional retail nursery, surrounded by living and breathing plants, we have switched to buying from high carbon footprint warehouses constructed of steel, bitumen and concrete.

The energiser of the common place garden. ▲

Who wants a common place garden?

Driving through our country towns can be a depressing experience these days.

The flight to the city of most of the working population is devastating the social fabric of small country towns, creating ghost-like dilapidated buildings where the only meal now offered is from the petrol station.

The car has also been responsible for the uprooting of avenues of trees that at the very least gave some aesthetic unity to the town's street scape.

Driving through our outer suburbs in the city ones senses are assaulted by the extreme vulgarity of gigantic McDonalds or KFC signage not to mention the hideous banner predation of a Harvey Norman or Bunnings store encouraging us to fill our homes with more gadgets.

The visual disharmony is reinforced by power lines, power poles and concrete. Trees which could soften this barrage are seemingly banned because they would interfere with our view of the signs. Is this a statement of our priorities? Corporate greed trumps public beauty.

What has this got to do with plants?

Well, the sort of plants that seem to fit in with this discordant sensory overload are the latest modern plant breeding from America; the ubiquitous bedding plants. They are effectively dwarf forms of traditional annuals but bred with enlarged flowers like modern marigolds.

These huge blobs of colour seem to be shouting "look at me" like a neon sign but what is even worse, most bedding annuals are offered in a bilious riot of colour that feels perfectly comfortable decorating the front of a fast food outlet.

But would you want such plants in your garden?

Traditional annuals which haven't been dwarfed or enlarged are still available, such as lupins, delphiniums and hollyhocks.

But nowadays 90% of the most common annuals like polyanthus, impatiens, petunias, pansies or sweet peas come in mixed colours or the flowers are only offered as enlarged doubles such as African marigolds.

The concept of carpet bedding can work brilliantly, as it does in well executed displays by local parks provided the colour combinations are well considered, but in front of a suburban home such striking colour arrangements become tiresome.

Colour is a device that has to be handled with restraint and subtlety which invariably excludes bedding plants and their advanced growing companions called potted colour.

TOP Clash of colours, ▲ forms and textures.

CENTRE Open day at breeder of modern bedding plants.

BOTTOM LEFT The subtlety of original carpet bedding at Wisley, UK.

BOTTOM RIGHT Modern plant bedding – enlarged flowers of vulgar colour clashes.

INSPIRING GARDENS

COASTAL GARDEN [Cold Zone 10   Heat Zone 4]

Heritage Australia • Heronswood Citation 1981

Built as a retreat by the academic and politician William Edward Hearn, to designs probably by Edward La Trobe Bateman, this picturesque Gothic Revival building is of national architectural importance, being an innovative and highly creative design.

The main house of 1871 is asymmetrically composed and constructed in bluestone with limestone dressings and bell-cast shaped roofs. The single story north east wing with varied windows and roof shapes, verandahs and loggia, contrasts with the more severe and conventional two-story south-west wings.

Heronswood

When I first saw Heronswood I was spellbound by its beauty

Its neo-gothic lines would become the perfect focal point for the creation of a garden my wife Penny and I wished for.

After just a few days living within its walls we developed such a respect for its creator, Edward La Trobe Bateman that we committed ourselves to its preservation, ensuring the garden complemented his vision.

Bateman, a cousin of Victoria's Governor, had studied architecture in London, worked for pre-eminent designer Owen Jones and assisted in designing the Crystal Palace in 1851.

A pre-Raphaelite who is largely forgotten today, he was "endowed with exquisite feeling and skill in decorative art, extremely rare at the time" said eminent literary figure, Mary Howitt.

"Bateman was the most talented and perhaps the most prolific Anglo-Australian landscape gardener of the 19th century" asserts Bill Bampton, the head gardener at Heronswood.

He produced designs for the University of Melbourne, Carlton, Fitzroy and Williamstown Botanic Gardens and Rippon Lea's first garden. Three of his buildings are listed on the register of national estate — HERONSWOOD at Dromana, BARRAGUNDA at Cape Schank and KOLOR at Penshurst.

The original Heronswood garden was a low maintenance garden protected from wind by Monterey cypress with a kikuya lawn. No plans exist to connect La Trobe Bateman with any garden design except the choice of Moreton Bay fig and the Cook Island pine, both of which were the typical evergreen trees he favoured.

The slab cottage with its rough hewn posts is thought to have been constructed with local eucalypts, which also provided posts for the main window frames of the house.

With granite blocks probably quarried 500m away on the Arthurs Seat ridge and limestone from the Mornington Peninsula, all of the Heronswood buildings were completely hand made with no connection to the industrial age.

The apron-like terrace at the north of the house and its steps leading past the Cook Island pine have an axial symmetry to the two holer outside toilet which is on a straight line through the front door to the front gate. We presume this design was inspired by La Trobe Bateman.

The Heronswood garden is on a ridge of Arthurs Seat with views west to Port Phillip Heads, and east across Shark Bay (now called Safety Beach) to Mount Martha. From the entrance to Heronswood, views of Melbourne's high rise buildings are visible on a clear day.

▲ LEFT The ducks of Heronswood.

RIGHT Using vegetables instead of obvious flowers to create garden beauty in the parterre.

We were fortunate when we arrived that the garden had some well chosen mature trees, such as the flame tree, *Gingko*, desert ash, two Himalayan cedars, a jelly palm and a Canary Island palm to provide vertical anchors to frame views of the sea which enabled us to create a cottage garden surrounding the house.

Our first task was to provide a pond for the 'Leunig' ducks we brought from Albert Park. Because of the steepness of the slope we created an axial walk across the site to link our vegetable parterre to the oak walk.

A private garden attached to the beautiful round room and shaded by the gigantic Moreton Bay fig with an infinity pool was completed in 1996 which echoed the roof structure of the main house.

Below the Cook Island pine we have planted a herb garden of rosemary patterns and medicinal herbs.

We constructed a restaurant in 1996 from low carbon intensive materials – with walls of rammed earth and a thatched roof of locally cut water reeds from the nearby Tootgarook swamp. Unfortunately a bushfire, started from a driver's cigarette and fanned by a southerly wind on 14th January 2014, destroyed the building except for a section of wall now retained as a folly.

The vegetable parterre

An Italian gardener would have terraced this steep slope but lack of funds prevented that.

We settled on a simple cut turf parterre in a circle with six segments. This created an inexpensive pattern on the lawn once the three seasonal plantings were finished each year and imposed a protocol of excluding untidy crops like pumpkins, tomatoes and melons whilst concentrating on foliage colours like Five Colour silverbeet in separate colours.

Inspired by the French chateau Villandry, we were determined to create an inexpensive vegetable garden every visitor to Heronswood could afford to recreate at home. Exquisitely beautiful colour and form from cabbages or upright form of leeks creates a vegetable garden of rare beauty.

HERONSWOOD'S CLIMATE & PLANT SELECTION

Cold Zone 10 • Frost free with a +4°C minimum, the same as Sydney, Adelaide and Brisbane.

Heat Zone 4 • 5-29 days over 30°C, the same as Albany, Sydney and Canberra.

Rainfall • 655mm. **Water Deficit** • 3-5 months.
Shade • Approximately 25%.

Trees • Drought tolerant, rainforest evergreens 80%, deciduous 20%.

Flowers • Evergreen perennials 50%, herbaceous perennials 40%, annuals 8%, bulbs 2% – Peak: November-April.

Our lawn

We inherited a kikuyu lawn which is drought tolerant and dependent on natural rainfall. From January to March, it is straw coloured but resprouts and is green from April-December. The gardeners have never used lawn fertiliser, simply mulching the grass back into the soil, oversown with lawn daisy to create a carpet of white in spring. In summer we raise the cutting blades to help shade the ground.

Our flowers PREDOMINANTLY HEIRLOOMS

It's what you exclude from your garden that defines its character particularly now most of the best heirloom flowers are rarely available in nurseries. Heronswood gardeners avoid mixed colour selections as these are rarely harmonious. We rarely plant potted annual colour because of their short flowering period or bedding colour, except in the parterre where they fit in well. We won't plant hybrid tea roses or floribunda roses, relying entirely on perennials and summer flowering shrubs. Indestructible diosmas and lomandras are great survivors but more suited to tough freeways than a selection for passionate gardeners.

Our food PREDOMINANTLY HEIRLOOMS

We have replaced camellia hedges with avocados and feijoas and have the biggest display of edibles – including sub-tropical fruit, Mediterranean fruit and heirloom vegetables – in Australia. We have integrated flowers, fruit and vegetables in a true cottager's style throughout the garden. The kitchen garden focuses on serving Diggers heirloom vegetables to our restaurant.

Our shade trees NATIVE EVERGREENS

The most important tree at Heronswood is the Moreton Bay fig. Not only is it a gigantic shade tree, it is a favourite for local kookaburras and a whole thriving ecosystem. Another of our favourites is *Ficus microcarpa* var. *hillii*, which has mid-green leaves that don't drop in summer. We have a shady avenue, the Ficus walk, that provides heat relief in the hotter months. The desert ash gives shade on the main lawn for garden visitors. It is a fascinating tree. Visiting children sway on it and it replaces the calamitous "eucalyptic", providing better shade and beautiful chartreuse green leaves early in spring.

Our season

Being surrounded by the water from the ocean and the bay provides an insulation blanket that effectively delays the onset of spring, which is

TOP **North view with ▲ Chinese tile replicated in apron parterre.**
BOTTOM **Our arid garden.**

two weeks later than Melbourne, and keeps our garden winter minimum temperature to +4°C.

The onset of hot northerly winds from inland Victoria are cooled as they cross the bay reducing summer temperature by about 6°C. However on scorching hot, windless days 40°C+ are reached. The spring garden peaks in October-November and Heronswood's summer garden is appealing from January until May.

Organic certification

Whilst Heronswood's climate is benign with no frost and minimal outback scorchers, the light sandy soil doesn't retain moisture as well as heavier sandy loams do.

This is resolved in many ways. All green matter is composted to be used as mulch to boost soil fertility. We only choose drought tolerant plants (one drip) to save water for fruit trees, vegetables and a few precious perennials. Flower beds are mulched in early spring to prevent weeds and retain moisture. The organic levels of the soil are 10-20 times that of typical Australian soil (herbaceous border 20-23%, vegetable parterre 20-24%, lawn 12% and succulent dry garden 3%).

Notable people of Heronswood

WILLIAM EDWARD HEARN (1826-1888) was Heronswood's first owner. An Irish immigrant, Hearn arrived in 1855 as one of the four original professors at the newly established University of Melbourne, where he was later appointed Dean of the Faculty of Law (1873) and Chancellor (1886).

Author of four books, he was also Chancellor of the Church of England's diocese of Melbourne, a QC and a member of the Legislative Council.

ALEXANDER SUTHERLAND (1852-1902), Heronswood's second owner was a pupil at Melbourne University, sharing the Shakespeare scholarship with H.B. Higgins. Famous for his works *History of Australia* (1877) and *Victoria and its Metropolis* (1888), both of which were probably written at Heronswood.

HENRY BOURNES HIGGINS (1851-1929) was Heronswood's third owner and a QC as well as a delegate to the convention for the Australian Constitution, Federal Attorney General (1904), Justice of High Court and President to the Arbitration Court.

He delivered the landmark Harvester Judgment which led to establishing a minimum wage. An Irish immigrant thought to be the "Henry Higgins" in *Pygmalion*. Brother-in-law to Chinese Morrison.

GEORGE ERNEST 'CHINESE' MORRISON (1862-1920) was an Australian adventurer, Peking correspondent for the *The Times* in London, participant in the Boxer Rebellion, political advisor to the last Chinese emperor and brother-in-law to H.B. Higgins. His feats included 'back-tracking' the Burke and Wills expedition, walking 2,043 miles from the Gulf of Carpentaria to Melbourne in 123 days, surviving a spear attack during an expedition in New Guinea and walking 3,000 miles across China into Burma.

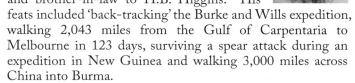

"Food prepared by the gardener"

Morrison spent Christmas at Heronswood in 1917. It was a forgettable gastronomic experience, as told in this extract from his diary.

"Breakfast at 9.15 and this is the country ... where one could breakfast at 7, a hearty hot meal. In this astonishing household we had a breakfast of burnt porridge and lukewarm eggs and literally sour bread with meagre helpings of tea doled out by my sister ...

Lunch was simply horrible. Remains of yesterday's cold beef cut in thin unappetising slices, potatoes in jackets and some dry cheese ...

Christmas dinner ... no wine was offered, and no whiskey, and there was found only one bottle of soda-water in this parsimonious house ... a shocking dinner ... a most deplorable experience.

Last day of this infernal food. Rejoice at the prospect of going tomorrow ... I am inadequately fed, and am offered food prepared probably by the gardener. I am in a constant state of irritation ... if people were poor curates to whom a three pence represented a coin worth saving I would say nothing, but to be invited to a house whose host is a Federal High Court Judge with ample earnings £2000 or £3000 a year, and to find that he and his wife ... are always seeking to save that three pence, is quite nauseating."

◄ The balcony tile that inspired the tile garden was similar to that displayed at the Crystal Palace in 1851.

◄ Opposite page
TOP The pool lawn at Heronswood.
BOTTOM LEFT The original 1864 slab cottage.
BOTTOM RIGHT Inside Heronswood's round room.

How rainforest trees saved Heronswood

The most important visual features at Heronswood are Edward La Trobe Bateman's neo-Gothic buildings that have continually inspired our garden endeavours.

His focus on rainforest evergreen trees appears to be still 150 years ahead of modern garden preferences.

We have created a garden to fit in with his buildings, using plants that were popular at that time before modern plant breeders destroyed their charm.

Climate change continues to threaten our gardening endeavours, making the shading of gardens more urgent, so using cooling effects of evergreens is even more important today.

The thatched roof restaurant

The fire that destroyed our restaurant was ignited by a cigarette butt thrown from a passing car along a freeway on a total fire ban day of over 40°C. It ignited the 'eucalyptic' tree (apologies to Phillip Adams) and created embers which lifted and fell on the thatch roof 400 metres away. The garden's saviour were the original plantings of Australian rainforest trees that stopped the bushfire caused by inflammable eucalypts.

The roof shape was our 1996 interpretation of La Trobe Bateman's design. Built from sustainable materials, the walls were constructed of rammed earth, the thatch roof from local *Phragmites australis* reeds cut from the Tootgarook swamp nearby.

Now all we have left is "The Folly" to stimulate our gardening endeavours.

La Trobe Bateman understood the danger 150 years ago but Australian gardeners are still ignoring the threat by planting eucalypts in their gardens.

The fire, driven by inflammable eucalyptus, catches hold of the thatch roof restaurant, Jan 2014

Building the rammed earth walls, 1996

Cutting reeds in the Tootgarook swamp

Tying the reeds into 'stooks'

German thatchers laying the roof

The restaurant the day before the fire

"The Folly" retained as a reminder

INSPIRING GARDENS

COUNTRY BUSH GARDEN   [Cold Zone 9b   Heat Zone 4]

St Erth

Headmaster Tommy Garnett transformed the bush and began his 2nd and 3rd careers

"Call me Tommy" was how my headmaster addressed me when, as a 36 year old former student, he befriended Penny and I after we started The Diggers Club. The Garden of St Erth was the creation of Tommy and Penny Garnett when they retired, aged 59, in 1974.

Tommy took an enormous interest in our gardening endeavours. He was happy to write for the struggling Diggers Club garden magazine. I couldn't believe my good fortune as I regard Tommy's writing as the most eloquent and informed in Australia's short garden history.

Getting to know Tommy was difficult for me as I was stuck in the headmaster-student mindset. He asked me up for lunch one day and during one of the many garden tours the phone rang. Tommy went inside to answer the call and he must have become distracted because he forgot that I was waiting outside. I hadn't the courage to knock on the door and so drove back to Melbourne.

Tommy had unbelievable energy. He started gardening at age four, but was interrupted for fifty-five years, being first a student at Charter House school, then Cambridge University and going on to become the headmaster of Marlborough College, then Geelong Grammar.

As a descendant of the famous Garnett family, better known in Australia through their involvement with "the Bloomsbury Set", Tommy combined his gardening and writing (his second and third careers) in a column in *The Age* titled "From the Country" for twelve years, which established him as one of Australia's foremost garden writers, and the author of six publications.

He restarted his garden career at age fifty-nine at the Garden of St Erth.

St Erth had the most unpromising soil which evolved out of miners' rubble. He and Penny would muck out horse stables every Friday and bring manure back to St Erth to literally create their own soil.

For many English migrants the bush was mysterious and frightening but for Tommy it was habitat for native birds and plants that he wished to study and it enabled him to explore how to plant his "English memories" in our harsh climate.

Their energy and commitment was truly awe-inspiring. When Tommy was too old to garden and finally retired he asked Penny and I to take over St Erth in 1996, and like a still-dutiful student, but now aged 52, I said yes. Tommy was an educator and communicator "par excellence" and proof that "three careers are better than one."

▲ LEFT Lupins in the border.

RIGHT The Food Forest combines perennial vegetables with fruit and nuts.

Tommy and I had much in common. We shared a passion for gardening and an interest in ecology. The fact that our wives were christened "Penelope" (meaning constant or faithful in Greek mythology) no doubt helped.

In his biography he describes how as a child he sat reading under a Jargonelle pear – not just any pear, but a Jargonelle pear.

His connection to the finest gardeners of the 20th century is described in his first article for the Diggers magazine. He came from the same village as the English cottage gardener Margery Fish.

The wife of Tommy's headmaster was a friend of Gertrude Jekyll, the famous garden collaborator to Edwin Lutyens. The notable garden designer Russell Page was a fellow student at Charterhouse School. Nearby were the famous gardens Tintinhull, Montacute, East Lambrook Manor and Barrington Court.

One of my favourite quotes of his is from his school teacher years is:

"Gardening gave way to running the school farm with no labour but that of the boys. There I learnt the valuable lesson that if you enjoy unskilled labour, the balance between Harm Done and Good Achieved is almost exactly even."

And later, when reflecting on his St Erth garden in Australia with its climatic differences and comparing his English experiences he wrote:

"In our present garden we call the pond a dam, trellis replaces the wall, the wood is the bush garden, and we have had to make an artificial stream."

His knowledge of Latin and interest in birds made the garden so special that when he retired he did not return in spite of writing "that a garden is never finished."

Tommy used the garden as a teaching ground for exploring his interest in native plants, dendrology, ornithology and particularly his interest in the effects of Australia's climate on winter hardiness of plants. He published his *Age* articles in book form as well as writing a biography of Alister Clarke.

When he finally parted from the Garden of St Erth, he asked The Diggers Club to buy the property and it became the cold climate outpost to our seaside companion- Heronswood garden.

The Diggers Club

Tommy and I both wanted Heronswood's head gardener, Dave Pomarre, to become head gardener at St Erth. Dave was one of the few gardeners in the country who could competently continue Tommy's legacy.

Dave made changes by installing a border in front of the miner's cottage. Diggers transformed the historic miner's cottage into a retail shop and the Garnett's house into a restaurant. This all happened in 1996. The focus on fruiting plants began in 2004 with an espaliered orchard, berry garden and our ode to permaculture with the food forest, which are all grown under organic certification.

In 2013 Andrew Laidlaw redesigned the Bush Walk and in 2014 the Daffodil Paddock was enhanced with plantings of roses and perennials.

I wanted Tommy's words to give a brief story of the garden during his time there.

The beginnings

"It was pelting with rain on a bitter mid-winter day in June when Penelope and I decided to buy it: if we liked it under these circumstances, we ought to be happy with it under fair skies!"

"Mathew Rogers ... built the sandstone cottage which he called after his birth place, the village of St. Erth in Cornwall."

"1967. The government department responsible for land tenure in mining areas advised that the area was totally unsuitable for a garden."

"In 1970 garden rooms were the height of fashion ... congenitally suspicious of garden "fashions" ... we were slightly mortified to have such rooms forced upon us."

"All the components of the first garden I can clearly visualise are present in our garden on the other side of the world not consciously imitated but perhaps imprinted like the calls of a mother duck."

"Penelope and I became self-sufficient in vegetables, which have always been her first love."

The English garden

"At the time of my retirement, my colleagues wished to buy me a present ... A deodar (cedar), a weeping mulberry, a tulip tree, a *Gingko* and a Dawn redwood *Metasequoia glyptostroboides*."

The bush garden

"At the beginning of 1974 we were conscious that we knew very little about native plants. Geoff Carr who had run a native nursery offered us the last of his stock – about seventeen hundred of them for just $300."

Garden prejudices

"What constitutes an acceptable combination of plants is a matter of taste. To my eye roses – though not rhododendrons – look utterly out of place with eucalypts. In general, gardeners' hybrids of any sort are better kept to their own company. Socialites look out of place at a bush picnic."

"The growing of natives gets mixed up with patriotism and exotics with home sickness."

Summary

"All gardening is based upon decay and renewal. The making of it has given happiness to those of us who have helped - and are still helping – to make it, and we like to believe to some of those who have watched it growing."

HEAD MASTER TO PRINCE CHARLES

Regarded as an ultra-liberal, as Headmaster at Marlborough Tommy introduced co-education which he repeated at Geelong Grammar. When asked by Sir Robert Menzies to become Headmaster for Prince Charles he replied *"he would have to interview his parents!"* Having been unhappy at Gordonstoun, there was concern but after the time at Timbertop, the Prince's Equerry said by way of approval *"I went out with a boy and came back with a man"*.

JEREMY FRANCIS is a master gardener who combines the unique talent of being a plantsman with a deep interest in garden design. Whilst farming two properties in Western Australia he was patiently awaiting the time to create his 'Great Garden'. Inspired by visiting Sissinghurst, Hidcote and Penelope Hobhouse's Tintinhull House, he planned his move carefully.

Jeremy chose the Dandenong Ranges because the soil was deep and fertile. The summer temperatures are 4-6 degrees cooler then Melbourne and the rainfall 1.2m a year, double that of the city. It paid off – after Melbourne's last heat wave of four days over 40°C he hasn't had to water at all! One doesn't normally think of Jeremy as ruthless but it is what he refuses to plant that distinguishes his garden. He is a perfectionist. Every plant has to pay its rent so plants that are short flowering, have poor foliage or form don't make his list. The garden is full of plants we would describe as garden-worthy!

He is disdainful about short, stumpy nonsense like dwarf alstroemerias which nurseries offer in preference to the tall, elegant butterfly flowers he is seeking. With Cloudehill being open to the public and subject to critical opinion every month of the year, it is vital that every plant contributes to the overall garden picture.

Cloudehill

Jeremy shares the four seasons at Cloudehill

I have lived most of my life in a part of Australia where gardening is almost impossible.

My family farmed two hours drive north of Perth in WA. Winters there were glorious, cool and moist and mild but summers ferocious, very hot, very dry, very windy. On top of that, there was little water. And what water there was had salt in it.

There were almost no gardens for a long way around. On the other hand, that farmland west of New Norcia, the Darling Escarpment hills of Mogumber and Gillingarra was, by the standards of WA farmland, very handsome country. And with the rain every winter it was magnificent.

So, I know about Mediterranean style gardening: summer aridity, heat and wind. And extreme Mediterranean gardening at that: Mogumber summers bear more resemblance to Algeria and Morocco than the oaken woodlands of the south of France. There are few gardens in that part of WA – my own was a local phenomenon.

Still, after 15 years making the most of it I was becoming ever more ambitious in the plants I was attempting to grow and eager to try gardening somewhere more congenial - hence the move to Olinda.

And now, 20 years on, chatting with gardeners from famous English gardens complaining of their stiff clay soil, unseasonable killing frosts, entire gardens raddled with honey fungus (Sissinghurst), I have come to appreciate the Dandenongs is just about the best place for gardening anywhere.

One of the glories of the hills hereabouts is the seasons. Summers can be so mild and moist they resemble a West Australian winter. Autumns are drier, generally cool and invigorating, certainly never bitter.

Neither is winter. Mist sometimes lies through the tree tops for days yet the temperature rarely slips below five degrees.

Mind you, it hardly rises above 12 either and we look forward to spring. And spring is (most of the time) glorious.

Cloudehill is made up of some 25 gardens. Each has its theme, character, planting, and its period of interest. The advantage of a garden of compartments is we can have things happening 12 months of the year.

Visitors should always find two or three of Cloudehill's garden rooms at their peak.

◄ TOP Pastel border.
BOTTOM Hot border.

▲ Bluebells adorn one of Cloudehill's meadows.

Spring

Beginning with spring we have bulb meadows. The bulbs in these rough grass areas were planted by Jim Woolrich as part of his flower farm business in the 30s. The bulbs have had generations to naturalise.

Our meadows commence flowering in July and August with early *narcissus* and grape hyacinths, bluebells and mid-spring bulbs bloom in September and October, South African bulbs and flowering grasses carry the show through to early summer. We slash the grass in February and nerines pop up in autumn. The great advantage of growing bulbs this way is the grass hides the bulbs' dying foliage. Spring is busy, as it should be in any temperate garden.

Lilacs in the shrub walk are flowering, rhododendrons everywhere (they were planted out in hedges by the Woolrichs 50 years back and these have been incorporated into the garden) and the glory of this season in Cloudehill are the bluebells. When people ask "when is the best time to visit in spring?" I reply "early October, with the beeches leafing out and the Spanish bluebells flowering". Beech foliage is translucent as it unfurls and we have a collection of photos by Claire Takacs of copper beech in fresh foliage with entire hillsides of bluebells spilling underneath. Several have won international awards.

Towards the end of spring we have peonies flowering. The Japanese are the first, then the American hybrids, the herbaceous, and finally the (recently available) intersectional hybrids. These last are crosses between herbaceous and tree peonies and have particularly sumptuous flowers. They also bloom for an extended period, have no chilling requirements to flower and perform happily in beachside gardens.

The shrub borders are full of colour by this time and what with Japanese maples in fresh leaf the overall effect is overpowering: perhaps just a bit busy. Or am I being purist? I do find this is a good time to prepare our summer borders and often ignore the rest of the garden.

Summer

Our summer borders are the highlight of Cloudehill. Their terrace cuts right across the width of the garden, vistas run out to more gardens above and below. Herbaceous perennials are largely why we are in the Dandenongs. Perennial borders are practical in much of Australia, the southern half at least, if plants are chosen carefully, but there are few herbaceous perennials that won't thrive in the Dandenongs.

Altogether, there are five gardens along this terrace, two devoted to perennials. Our first pair of borders are devoted to warm colours: yellows, reds, oranges, the second the cooler colours. Visitors, so long as they explore the way I want them to, discover the warm borders first and are teased by a glimpse of misty mauves and pastels through two central brick archways. The principal is that the soft colours emphasise the length of the terrace and exaggerate the size of the garden.

We use several hundred different plants with as many late season flowering varieties as possible to give a long season of interest. The borders commence flowering late November and build through to Christmas and hold their themes pretty-well through to mid-march. They are still worth seeing in autumn mind you, for their bleaching colours and tawny seed heads. And by that time there is autumn colour elsewhere.

Cloudehill

89 Olinda-Monbulk
Road, Olinda
VIC 3788

Open daily 9-5

Seasons Restaurant
03 9751 0168

Diggers Garden Shop
Rare & advanced plants
03 9751 0584

Autumn

The great joy of working on a property which has been famous for three generations now is the historic trees and shrubs.

European beech are everywhere, some 90 years old; also rhododendrons, several huge Himalayan tree rhododendrons around our restaurant for instance but two Japanese weeping maples are the most important plants in the garden.

They are simply awe inspiring, world class specimens. They came from Japan in 1928, sent from the famous Yokohama Trading Nursery to Ted Woolrich as he was establishing his Rangeview Nursery. We dug them with extreme care and planted them on the main terrace and made the entire garden around them.

Their leaves emerge aubergine-crimson in spring, gradually soften in the warmer months and flare to silken orange-red for two or three weeks in April.

Winter

Always my favourite season on the farm in WA. And I still rather enjoy a bit of wild windy June weather in the Dandenongs, perhaps keeping an eye of the thermometer for snow. June is the test of a garden: no colour at all, does the architecture hold it together?

Early on we decided beech should be the symbol of Cloudehill. We already had rows of them, big trees 50 and 70 years old.

It was very tempting to plant formal beech hedges. They make the best possible hedge. Just a couple of years back I needed a screen around our new Commedia dell'Arte Lawn and, crikey, there was nothing for it.

So we planted yet another beech hedge, just a plain green one this time. Visit some June morning with sun coming through the mountain mist and hedges everywhere rustling with coppery dry leaves and you will see why.

▲ Autumn colours of beech.

Winter snow. ▼

GARDEN SOLUTIONS

Garden selections to create the uncommon garden

Choosing plants carefully

Permanence: Choosing subtle and garden-worthy perennials

Colour schemes for your garden

Forget spring, summer is the season

Foliage contrasts in the Heronswood herb garden. ▲

▲ Tying in Heronswood's summer border with the house.

◄ Heronswood's herb garden and lotus pond, with cooling effects of lush, green foliage.

Garden selections to create the uncommon garden

▲ LEFT **The grey foliage of Russian olive.**

CENTRE **Cape chestnut.**

RIGHT **Smoke bush.**

It is always easy to criticise other gardens and much harder to actually create a garden that would be universally admired.

So what I will do is begin the discussion about the sort of plants that I would choose, if instead of living in a beautiful historic house with three acres of garden I were living in the suburbs in a cream brick veneer with a quarter acre block for a garden. Assuming the garden has about 200 square metres of sunny space, I would provide a shade to sun ratio of 20:80 and within that sunny growing area provide beds for fruit and vegetables (25%), flowers (40%) and lawn (15%).

Trees for shade (20% of area)

The most important decision after you have worked out what you want from your garden is to choose the trees. In keeping with my desire to ensure the garden looks its best in summer rather than spring I would choose two trees that complement each other by providing good foliage contrast as well as excellent shade.

My first choice would be a cape chestnut because of its lush green foliage which not only provides cool shade but also because of its handsome summer flowers; a light pink or white selection. Near but separately from the cape chestnut I would plant a Russian olive because of its graceful weeping habit, its fragrant spring scented blooms and because the combination of foliage contrast of the green and the grey looks elegant together.

Both of them will grow well in low rainfall, are not too tall or out of balance with the house and survive without much additional summer watering. There would be plenty of room for citrus trees and fruit trees which would be pruned to picking height but that would be a matter of personal choice. Whilst the trees would be placed to visually anchor the house, it is the shrubberies that can be used to tie the living plants and trace the beds and paths to the house.

If the bricks were not a colour that integrated with the garden then I would clothe the walls in Virginia creeper which provides a lovely green backdrop in summer and then magnificent red autumn foliage before dropping its leaves in early winter. There are so many shrubs to choose from but perhaps it is best to start by discussing those I would avoid.

Shrubs

Any shrub that is spring flowering like azaleas and rhododendrons I would exclude in favour of a shrub with less colour and greater subtlety such as the smoke bush. Its green form has the lightest green foliage and then the tiniest insignificant flowers that envelope the foliage in summer clouds of airy white then return to green and in a final act provide striking autumn colour. Smoke bush combines with, and enhances, all its neighbours rather than being a soloist like an azalea which is then is exhausted during summer. Some would swap an azalea for a blueberry in that both enjoy shade and an acid soil followed by striking autumn colour.

I would also find a place for the angels trumpet, not just because of its exquisite perfume but for its repeat flowerings through its growing season and the spectacular hanging blooms – reminiscent of a visiting flock of birds.

You might have a weakness for a camellia but let me dissuade you. The avocado we buy in the supermarket grows in a similar position and climate so wouldn't you rather have fifty or more avocados hanging from branches until the fruit is ready to pick? It grows in shady spots which are well watered (in every capital city except Canberra). It may not be as elegant as a camellia but the sheer joy of picking your own fruit makes up for that.

Fruit and vegetables together (25% of area)

My vegetable garden would be surrounded by mini-fruit trees such as oranges, grapefruit and lemons for the scent of their flowers, the lushness of their evergreen leaves, as well as their fruit. There are no better companions for planting in a vegetable garden than dwarf citrus and espaliered apples and pears as everyone who visits Heronswood will testify.

I would also find space for that citrus relative *Murraya paniculata* because of its beautiful white highly perfumed flowers as well the rarely planted Nagami kumquat. Most nurserymen push gardeners towards the pseudo kumquat Calamodon which has pips and sour fruit unlike the Nagami which has edible skin and much sweeter fruit which can be eaten out of hand.

Climbers

I know everyone loves the wisteria vine particularly when grown over a long rounded arch which, when in full bloom, has thousands of flowers all hanging and swaying in the spring breeze. But consider that this wisteria will look dull and untidy in summer, just when visitors come for the holidays in summer.

Far better to choose a summer fruiting or flowering vine such as *Solanum wendlandii*. The lush green foliage is cooling on the brightest day and its large light blue flowers are a perfect colour on a hot summer's day and its flowers last from December through to May. I would give it plenty of room perhaps 3-4 metres of pergola or support for it to ascend a north facing wall.

I would construct a pergola just for a muscatelle grape to provide cooling shade and the most memorable flavour of any dessert grape. If your trees are too small to provide shade in the early years of your garden development then a grape arbour needs to constructed because the grape will smother it in 1-2 years.

Heirloom flowers (30% of area)

For flowers I would create a little summer border which is the most difficult but the most creative and satisfying part of gardening that I've ever done. The border would need to face north east rather than west. This would provide protection from the hottest afternoon sun late in the day.

My border would be 12.5 metres long and 4 metres deep. It would require about 450 herbaceous plants. It would have space for unimproved delphinium Blue Sensation, achillea, coneflower, sedum, agastache and lots of grey foliage plants. Each would be bought in quantities of ten or twenty so that all up there would be about twenty to fifty different varieties of plants

Ephemerals (10% of area)

Amongst the all too brief flowering ephemerals I would find space for Flanders poppy with its mesmerising cups of blood red flowers in spring. A magnificent sight amongst the olive groves in Tuscany but I would be content finding a sunny dry spot which would also suit the deliciously scented *Freesia refracta alba*.

I would also find space for two charmers with but fleeting displays – the rare and charming blue-green *Ixia viridiflora* and the peacock flower *Morea aristata*. Amongst the lawn would be greenish trumpet daffodils Rus Holland so that they didn't spoil the border. Most gardeners are enticed into planting tulips in their backyard but let me tell you why this is such a bad idea.

Why not tulips?

They may be as beautiful as a lotus flower but they are a very expensive mistake nearly all gardeners make. They only flower for 2-3 weeks then the petals fall off and a forlorn stump is left that must be protected for another 8 weeks before it can be lifted. So it takes up space that should have been planted with summer flowers such as annuals or perennials.

Tulips need hot dry soil, as it was in their native Turkey. Should you forget where your tulips are and over plant, they get watered and rot and their ever so brief flowering turns into a mushy failure.

So what to recommend instead?

I would devote my energies into planting cabbages! They have the most sublime coloured foliage and form of any plant and they are extraordinary to watch on cold, frosty or sunny days. It is not just the heads but the curling outer leaves of any savoy or blue cabbage (really in fact a purple form) and a cultivar January King.

Now I know that this is a radical idea but if you can see the beauty in a humble cabbage then my guess is you are not going to create a commonplace garden.

TO HELP WITH PLANNING YOUR SPACE, SEE PAGES 60-61.

▲ *Freesia refracta alba.*　　　　　Pink peony poppies. ▼

▲ Heirloom drumhead cabbages.　　　　　Flanders poppies. ▼

Looking out across ▲
Port Phillip Bay from
Heronswood house.

The importance
of grey foliage
in linking blue
sea, blue sky
and contrasting
green foliage
perennials.

◀ LEFT Summer foliage
contrasts and herbaceous
flowers.

RIGHT Spring companions
– olives and echiums.

27

Choosing plants carefully

The pictures here are carefully chosen
to highlight the challenges of using the
flowers we love to create garden pictures of
long-lasting beauty!

The picture of a modern, brick and tile suburban house
(right) shows coloured permanent foliage and bold
forms integrating the house and garden, with annual
flowers providing only ten percent of the picture frame.

The ghastly suburban garden picture (below left)
has no permanence, lacking form or foliage to carry
interest for 12 months. The colours of the flowers
have to fit in a picture frame where the roof tiles and
the brick colours are predominant because there are no
bulky physical forms other than the letter box. The eye
is forced to focus on hot coloured bricks.

Short lived annuals

Annuals need to be a minor element,
not the total picture.

Typical parks bedding display that
looks stunning but if copied at home
would tire the senses.

This bedding display highlights the
sensory overload from modern bedding
colour with flower size too large and
colours such as red, blue and yellow all
mixed in together.

Permanent perennials

The most popular single colour garden
– the 'White Garden' at Sissinghurst –
works because the white flowers contrast
against a green background. The white
and grey foliage confined within a box
hedge are cool and refreshing.

A warmer two colour version with
yellow annual marigolds, softened with
grey permanent santolina and enclosed
by green box. The ideal way to use
bedding, with about 30% annuals as
ephemerals and 70% perennials.

Simple use of two colours of
permanent perennials with achillea
Moonshine and trachelium. Picture
is pleasing and harmonious because
flowers are subtle.

Exuberant cottage poppies and lupins (right) are two colours of contrast – opposite on the colour wheel. A pleasing picture enhanced by a vertical form of lupins to balance the globular shape of Oriental poppies.

Sadly the display lasts two weeks at most and needs three-dimensional foliage plants such as grey evergreens and longer flowering perennials to turn a pleasing image into a pleasing garden.

As gardeners build knowledge and experience of flowers they like, they'll learn to choose good two-dimensional plants with contrasting foliage or form. An Australian flower garden needs to be appealing for eight months not two to four weeks. Luckily, this is can be achieved with careful plant selection.

Grey foliage plants contrast beautifully with green foliage and green lawns and they almost always survive hot dry summers and knit pastel perennial flowers into harmonious pictures well.

In fact, grey is the most important foliage colour in our Heronswood garden, highlighting pink, blue and cream coloured flowers.

In tropical climates or where overcast skies favour the use of hot coloured flowers, bronze foliage knits hot coloured flowers nicely, but grey and bronze together look out of place.

The **PLANT FORM SELECTOR** below groups plants into forms or foliage irrespective of flower colour.

PLANT FORM SELECTOR – Choosing flowering plants for form and foliage

FLOWERS – Single dimension colours		Flower varieties to select (EV = evergreen)
Colour highlights but open, usually shapeless, form. Display is monotonous without vertical, spiky and mounded forms.		Coneflower, oriental poppy, penstemon, coreopsis, aster (autumn flowering), gaillardia, rudbeckia, dahlia, *romneya*, delphinium, gaura, phlox and agastache.
Vertical, see-through varieties give borders an added airy third dimension.	‖‖‖	Achillea (yellow, red, white, orange & purple flowers), *Verbena bonariensis*, *Thalictrum*, Russian sage (grey foliage), *Echinops*, *Eryngium* and agapanthus (EV).

FORMS – Second and third dimensions		Flower varieties to select
Solid verticals	‖‖‖	**Summer flowering:** hollyhocks, verbascum Wedding Candles, verbascum Banana Custard, canna, *Agastache rugosa* and angelica. **Spring flowering:** foxgloves, lupins, clary sage and *acanthus*.
Mounded foliage	⌂	Sedum, artemisia Powis Castle (grey foliage) and *Helichrysum petiolare* (grey foliage).
Spiky forms – Contrast with mounds. Most are evergreen, giving tubular, green texture.	⦚⦚	**Grasses** (EV): *Stipa gigantea*, *Miscanthus sp.*, *Pennisetum rubrum*, *Pennisetum setaceum*, *Elegia capensis*, *Panicum virgatum*, Daylilies (EV), *Phormium tenax* (EV), *Crocosmia sp.*, *Astelia chathamica*, (grey, EV), *Dierama sp.* and red hot pokers (EV).

FOLIAGE – Second and third dimensions		Flower varieties to select
Grey foliage provides good contrast to predominant green. Thrives in heat and dry conditions. Needs up to 25% of planting under Australian skies.		Wormwood Valerie Finnis, catmint *(Nepeta sp.)*, lamb's ears (spreading habit), artichoke/cardoon, lavender cotton, *Senecio serpens* (blue foliage), gysophila, dianthus, *Ballota pseudodictamnus* and tree wormwood.

Permanence: Choosing subtle and garden-worthy perennials

▲ LEFT AND CENTRE Lotus is an ultimate 3 dimensional plant, with outstanding foliage form and intriguing flowers, not to mention its distinctive seed pods.

RIGHT Lamb's ears have subtle flowers but woolly, textural leaves of grey to contrast with green foliage.

As gardeners, most of us are striving in our gardens to create beautiful garden pictures. All of us at some time have been seduced by the nursery's latest new plant or new colour form, only to find out later that when the plant finishes flowering it leaves a large ugly space in our picture frame.

Without exception, the most popular and commercially successful plants have been what I call 'one dimensional', being flowers whose plants have no form or foliage to give visual appeal once flowering has finished. The list is so long it is almost endless. In the case of bedding plants think of petunias, marigolds, sweet peas and impatiens. For shrubs think of azaleas and rhododendrons, as well as modern hybrid tea roses.

As gardeners build up their knowledge and experience they invariably progress beyond the ephemeral high impulse one-dimensional plants such as bedding annuals and opt for perennials which once planted live for three or more years, many living beyond five years. Creating a beautiful garden with perennials is a high art form expressed successfully by some of the greatest gardeners such as Vita Sackville-West at Sissinghurst, Christopher Lloyd at Great Dixter and Lawrence Johnston at Hidcote. Jeremy Francis' garden at Cloudehill is an outstanding Australian example.

New Zealand flax is a classic upright evergreen perennial that has won so much favour recently it has become tiresome and gardeners should consider other perennials such as achilleas, gunneras, acanthus and even the hanging form of rosemary to cover a wall. Unfortunately few of our native shrubs retain their good form throughout the year but *Richea pandanifolia* from the forests of Tasmania would win the Oscar if I were the judge.

Two dimensional selections

Of course every perennial border has a few "must have" exuberant specimens such as Blue Sensation delphiniums, coneflowers, poppies and liliums but these ephemerals must be planted next to hard working two-dimensional plants with good foliage, particularly the greys of wormwoods, rue, lamb's ears, santolina, sages and Russian sage.

Three dimensionals

The ultimate flowering perennial with outstanding flowers, appealing foliage and form is sadly committed to water only. The lotus comes closer to perfection than any other (perennial) and we are delighted to say we have a small but beautiful pond at Heronswood to enjoy on its own and without perennial companions. Perennial gardeners must make do with other choices, such as sedum Autumn Joy which, like the coneflower, is constantly changing with the seasons.

No other herbaceous perennial I know can hold the spotlight continuously from January to May. Lamb's ears, with its amethyst flowers and whorly texture that is so appealing, is too subtle to become first choice for most people; rather it works like a social networker enhancing the beauty of all its neighbours.

The over planted agapanthus is probably the best example of a three dimensional plant that is familiar to all gardeners. It usually displays best on its own but its exquisitely beautiful flower spikes have a vertical, see-through quality, enhanced by evergreen strap-like leaves.

It is useful to split the range of perennials into three groupings, just like our Heronswood gardeners do.

EVERGREEN PERENNIALS that don't retreat underground in winter providing twelve months of interest.

They are grown for their foliage rather than their flowers and make a fascinating tapestry in every way as appealing as a 'bush garden'.

Evergreen perennials have a border on their own and include wigandia, flax, *astelia*, *romneya*, echium, *senecio*, honey bush, scented geraniums, variegated and purple sage and grasses. All are drought tolerant one-drip plants for capital cities and coastlines that can tolerate a light frost (CZ 9b, 10, 11).

HERBACEOUS PERENNIALS have permanent roots and annual flowering stems. Flowers and foliage re-emerge in spring. At Heronswood multi-dimensional achilleas, sedums, Russian sage and wormwood hold together spectacular one-dimensional delphiniums, coneflowers, agastache and *Salvia nemorosa*. They are mostly 1 drip (drought tolerant) plants, coming from heavy frost areas of the northern hemisphere (CZ 8-10).

SUBTROPICAL TEXTURAL PLANTS are evergreen and give twelve months unchanging display with striking bold foliage such as *Yucca desmetiana*, *Aeonium velour*, *Kalanchoe pumila*, agave nova and *Lobelia aberdarica* (CZ 10-11). Agapanthus, lavender and lotus all generally look best on their own as focal highlights.

If you come to Heronswood you will see it all.

LEFT **Textural colours ▲** from sage.

CENTRE **The dramatic form** of the Dragon tree.

RIGHT **Vertical candles of** blue, evergreen *Echium candicans.*

LEFT *Artemisia arborescens* ▼ 'Powis Castle'.

RIGHT **Californian Tree Poppy.**

Colour schemes for your garden

How many times have you bought plants on impulse only to plant them in your garden and be disappointed because the flower colours clash?

Just as colour selections can create the right mood inside the house they need to be handled intelligently outside! The prevailing colour in Australian gardens is usually provided by a green lawn, a dull khaki green canopy of trees and a blue sky in summer.

At Heronswood we enjoy views over Port Phillip Bay so our foreground is sometimes the blue of water and also the blue sky.

Because the house is constructed of limestone, grey coloured granite and slate roof tiles, the prevailing colours that links a harmonious picture together are grey and blue. Grey foliage contrasts with the green lawn and blue light links the sky, the sea and the house together.

Over years of experimenting with colour we have formed some clear rules that work best in the bright light of the harsh Australian sun. This of course is totally different to the overcast grey skies of English summer gardens featured in the English books Australians look to for guidance.

Hot colours are warming

Colour is all about balance. In winter and spring with overcast skies and chilly winds the hot colours – the yellow of daffodils, or the red of tulips or Flanders poppies are thrilling and uplifting.

Pastel colours are cooling

But during hot summers with bright sunny skies bright colours become tiring – reinforcing the unpleasantness of the heat. We prefer to avoid hot coloured plants in summer and plant the perennial border with pastel colours – such as light blue, pink, grey, pale yellow and creams.

We also find white doesn't integrate with pastels so we confine white coloured perennials to their own separate garden.

If we lived in the UK where cloudy skies are normal throughout summer and temperatures rarely exceed 25°C then hot colours would be stimulating and thrilling as they are uplifting in our spring.

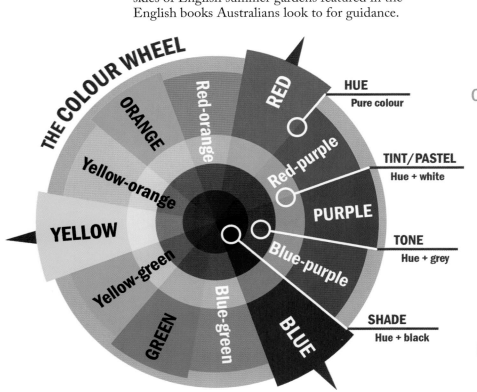

THE COLOUR WHEEL

ORANGE · Red-orange · RED · Red-purple · PURPLE · Blue-purple · BLUE · Blue-green · GREEN · Yellow-green · YELLOW · Yellow-orange

HUE — Pure colour

TINT/PASTEL — Hue + white

TONE — Hue + grey

SHADE — Hue + black

Choose HOT colours between red and yellow on the colour wheel

Choose COOL colours between green and purple

Create colour HARMONIES with adjacent colours

Create colour CONTRASTS with opposite colours

Create PASTELS by mixing a pure hue with white

As a general rule we avoid even using dots of bright red in our pastel border. However we do use red and vibrant yellows throughout our vegetable garden because of the preponderance of green from the lawn (not khaki eucalyptus greens), the leaves of our vegetables and citrus trees are also cooling, whereas greys and pastels are timid and ineffectual.

At the back of our house where a gigantic Moreton Bay fig dominates with its branched, brown trunk and flat, green leaves we also plant vibrant dahlias with crimson or egg-yellow flowers so we can enjoy every different coloured flower in our garden but never in the same visual frame or the same season.

Colour theory is a complex issue made more confusing for gardeners by the impact of heavy or light physical plant forms. Of course every gardener must choose what suits their garden, their trees and the modern tones of bricks or woodwork to create their own pleasing harmonies.

We have provided a colour wheel to help you understand the rules of colour.

Hot colours Red, orange, yellow — adjacent colours on the colour wheel share a yellow pigment and, planted together, create harmonies.

Cool colours Green, blue, violet — adjacent colours on the colour wheel – share a blue pigment and are harmonious together creating a calming influence.

By keeping hot colours together or cool colours grouped together, pleasing harmonies are created.

As gardeners become more skilled they can create striking effects by choosing colours opposite to each other.

These combinations are exciting two colour combinations but become discordant when other colours are used (white contains all other colours). Whilst grey and white are not part of the colour wheel they are still important colours to use.

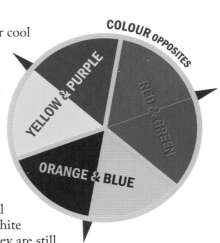

COLOUR OPPOSITES
YELLOW & PURPLE
RED & GREEN
ORANGE & BLUE

▲ The white garden at Heronswood contrasts with a green and grey Russian olive.

Single colour gardens that were created by Vita Sackville-West at Sissinghurst, famous for its White Garden, are really a contrast of white against green with grey foliage to break the monotony. White iceberg roses planted within green box hedges is an Australian adaption which is simple even if it is austere when carried through exclusively, but the impact is cool and refreshing against our hot sun.

Some of the world's most talented gardeners have variations on green themes with shiny and dull foliage, light greens and dark greens. Some, such as those found in Oriental gardens, are so effective that we admire them for being restful and contemplative.

In most situations, the more colours that are planted in a garden, the less pleasing the result. *Mature and experienced gardeners handle colour with respect and moderation.*

TOP The hot colours of ▶ red Ladybird poppy are softened by grey Tuscan kale and green foliage.

BOTTOM Hot colours look striking on bronze foliage.

INSPIRING GARDENS

ROYAL BOTANIC GARDENS MELBOURNE

▲ Guilfoyle's volcano – a perfect picture of form and foliage.

The Children's Garden. ▼

Forget spring, summer is the season

The greatest weakness in Australian gardens is that gardeners focus is on spring peaks so that when summer comes the garden is dull, out of shape and looking tired.

But if we ventured into famous botanic gardens in summer, gardeners would be stimulated by the elegant flowering shrubs, refreshed by the coolness of the shade trees and the lushness of the lawns.

Why is it so?

It is simply a question of choosing plants that peak in summer rather than spring. If you venture into a nursery when the weather warms it will be full of plants that display well at this time.

We would find azaleas, camellias, peonies, rhododendrons, lilac, wisteria, cistus and jasmine all looking inviting, tempting us to buy but if we did, then our garden would be flat and uninteresting throughout summer.

We are unlikely to find plants of buddleja, *brugmansia*, *romneya*, hydrangea, smoke bush, custard apple or pomegranate which all look magnificent in summer.

Unfortunately many domestic and display gardens focus on the spring season first and summer displays are secondary. There are only a few gardens that can guide you in planning for long summer interest.

Choosing garden-worthy plants that have appeal because of foliage or form rather than flowers provides one of the solutions. Fruiting plants produce flowers and fruits during summer such as pomegranate, blueberry and persimmon.

Below is a list of structural plants that we use at Heronswood to produce a summer focused garden. We have used a extraordinary range of trees of which about 30% are rainforest evergreen natives and less than 10% are deciduous exotics.

We have excluded eucalypts because of their shapelessness, falling debris, poor shade, arid look and inflammability. Our focus on exotic evergreens gives the garden good structure throughout the year and excellent shade on hot days and a cooling effect because of our focus on choosing trees with lush green foliage that have excellent drought tolerance.

Trees for summer shade

All these trees have thrived with natural rainfall and no additional watering and have reached generous proportions:

Moreton Bay fig, desert ash, Himalayan cedar, *Araucaria columnaris*, Queensland box, ginkgo, Canary Island palm, jelly palm, Atlantic cedar, Russian olive, juniper Hollywood, Irish yew, flame tree, pin oak, ombu, olive, holm oak, cork oak, *Ficus hillii*.

Hedges for summer

Myrtus communis subsp. tarentina, feijoa, avocado, natal plum, box, rosemary.

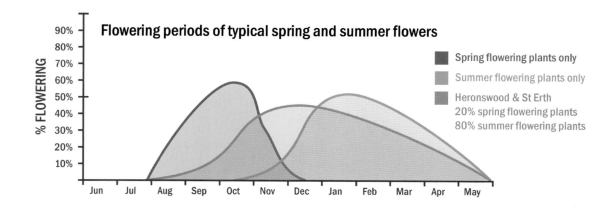

LEFT Cooling shade on hot ▲
days is provided by *Ficus hillii* at Heronswood.

RIGHT The shade canopy of desert ash frames Heronswood's summer perennial border.

Shrubs for summer

Wigandia, *romneya*, *brugsmansia*, honey bush, *Phlomis*, *Buddleja salvifolia*, tree gardenia, broom, rosemary, lavender, *Pseudopanax ferox*, *Murraya paniculata*, citrus including lemon, grapefruit, orange and kumquat.

After we have strengthened our planting of summer peaked plants there will still be room for winter and spring flowering plants such as magnolia, daphne, and wisteria, plus winter shade loving gems such as hellebores, primroses and foxgloves but, because there are more spring flowering plants in nurseries than summer flowering, it is vital to restrain this planting proportion to about 1/3 of the planted area.

Relying on summer borders for stimulation

Having travelled extensively through England, America, Holland and France visiting gardens, the supreme gardening achievement is undoubtedly the English summer border. It is a breathtaking experience to walk along a border and hear the buzzing of bees scrambling for nectar from flowering plants up to 2 metres tall.

With a long wall as a background behind, all the perennials are beautifully coordinated for colour, shape and form which is an extraordinary artistic achievement as complex in the visual arts as creating a musical symphony.

Nearly 100 years ago English plant collectors combed the world for perennial plants that thrived in their mild summers. They discovered a huge range, but probably only 10% of them are good performers under hot Australian summer skies. But enough to emulate borders and succeed under much tougher conditions.

Australia has hardly any native herbaceous plants that have developed perennial roots and annual flowering stems that can handle the move from cool alpine conditions to 30°C summer days – so nearly all our chosen perennials are from the lower alps in USA and Europe.

Finding adaptable perennials has been a mission of The Diggers Club for every year of our existence, not only to be able to survive, but thrive, with very little water.

These tough and garden-worthy plants are the flowering features at the gardens of Heronswood and St Erth and also at Cloudehill, even though summer perennial borders are rarely practised by Australian botanic gardens (except in Melbourne).

Our borders start with the emergence of foliage, usually in October, and many rise to 1.5 metres tall in just two months.

When foliage contrasts are well executed a tapestry of grey foliage and bronze should balance the greens before flowering begins in November. This is how borders can be visual features two months before and after flowering, extending the appeal from November to April.

The optimum planting regime to provide an extended period of interest is to use spring flowering plants in parts of the garden to create early spring interest but rely on perennials for most of the interest over summer.

This overcomes the problem of a flower bed devoted to spring flowers tiring by December, by which time it will be too late to plant summer flowering perennials. These need to be planted by August 30 at the latest to get established.

CREATING BEAUTY

WITH UNIMPROVED ORNAMENTALS

Planting herbaceous heirloom perennials

Planting evergreen perennials – an alternative to natives

Choosing garden-worthy trees and shrubs

Planting garden-worthy shrubs and roses

Ephemeral fillers – bulbs

Ephemeral fillers – heirloom annuals and biennials

Step-by-step sowing

Sowing wildflowers

Blue is the prime colour link at Heronswood. ▲

◄ Simple grasses, water and shade trees link the house and sky from Heronswood's viewing deck.

Planting herbaceous heirloom perennials

▲ Heronswood's summer perennial border is planted with heirloom perennials and looks appealing from November to April.

The English flower gardens that Australian travellers continually hunger for were created in the middle of the last century and reached their ultimate expression at Lawrence Johnston's Hidcote garden and Vita Sackville-West's Sissinghurst Castle.

Natives versus exotics

With an extraordinary selection of perennial flowering plants that thrive through frosty winters and coolish summers, no country in the southern hemisphere (except perhaps New Zealand) is blessed with good consistent rainfall and cloudy skies that sharpen the flower colours to create unforgettable floral impacts.

However there are many garden adaptations that will lift Australian spirits despite intense heat, poor soils and water limitations.

Many of Australia's native plants are of course perfectly adapted to extreme heat and drought. Over thousands of generations native shrubs, both low and medium sized, have survived by evolving woody stems. These shrubs have tough foliage and flower mostly in the cooler months of winter and spring.

Their virtue is their evergreen foliage and ability to survive in soils low in phosphorus and carbon.

However very few Australian natives have the spectacular summer flowers of northern hemisphere herbaceous perennials such as delphinium, lupin, coneflower and hollyhock. All of which are adapted to more fertile soil and have soft, fleshy foliage spurred on by extreme cold.

These herbaceous perennials retreat underground in winter thereby building up energy stores for rapid and spectacular flowering in summer.

Why are there so few native perennials?

Unfortunately Australia has a tiny range of herbaceous perennials compared with other continents. In our hot climate, woody stems of sub-shrubs predominate. Similarly in Mediterranean areas woody stemmed rosemary and lavender dominate.

There are extensive selections of Australian herbaceous perennials in frosty alpine areas but they would not grow successfully in lower altitudes where many of us garden.

Creating the summer border

The pinnacle of artistic flower gardening is the summer perennial border. No other form of gardening is so complex yet thrilling and satisfying. To be effective it requires blending an ultimate understanding of flowers, foliage and form, with a wonderful sense of colour and timing.

Seeing the shapes
Many of our favourite flowers have a form about as shapely as the overweight middle-aged. Charming they may be, but don't place them at the front of a picture you wish to create! Gauras and *Salvia azurea* are the two perennials that spring to mind: each would be wonderful in a natural garden but too floppy for a shapely summer border.

Three-dimensionals
These are the backbone of a summer herbaceous border with flowers pointing vertically to the sky giving the petals a see-through, three-dimensional quality.

Achillea, coneflower and bergamot are the most ethereal perennials, but the ultimate mainstay is *Verbena bonariensis* whose vertical scaffolding is even more intriguing than its flowers.

Spiky uprights Like mini-exclamation marks, with upright forms that dominate the landscape, these are a favourite choice of gardeners. In the herbaceous border use grasses such as miscanthus and *Stipa gigantea*, as well as crocosmia and kniphofia.

Mounding plants Plants of this kind are often sold in 150mm pots in nurseries, and are the only perennials available in nurseries that could be used in a summer border. Shasta daisy and penstemons are obvious choices but aster, phlox and scabiosa are also appropriate.

Place a double marigold amongst these subtle charmers, with its lairy, 'in your face' flowers, and you'll understand why perennial gardeners invariably become marigold bashers!

Verticals Verticals such as astelias, agastaches, delphiniums and verbascums can be used to contrast with mounding plants but shouldn't be placed next to spiky uprights because of their repetitive form.

Structurals Sedum, cannas and grasses bring solid foliage forms that hold the less shapely, long-flowering gaillardias and three-dimensional plants together.

Choosing foliage Because most flowering plants have green foliage, a border chosen for flowers alone can become shapeless and monotonous. Contrasting foliage is essential for visual relief.

However choosing plants for foliage requires restraint and a discerning eye, for they must provide a subtle contrast to the soothing green; if the contrast is too dominant, as it is in many suburban gardens, it creates visual disturbance.

Grey and silver foliage Foliage of this kind tends to illuminate neighbouring colours, particularly pastel pinks, blues and creams. Silver-foliaged plants cope with heat and drought better and thrive in full sun.

Low-growing border perennials with grey and silver foliage include *Achillea clypeolata*, *Artemisia* Valerie Finnis and Powis Castle, catmint, dianthus and lamb's ears. Summer shrubs in this category include curry plant, *Helichrysum petiolare* and wormwood, while grass-like examples include blue fescue, blue oat grass and *Stipa gigantea*.

Purple/bronze foliage This soaks up bright colours, particularly reds and violets, and can contrast with silver and green foliage, provided it is used sparingly.

The border dahlias like Bishop of Llandaff (red), Le Coco (yellow with red centre), Mt Noddy (velvet red) and Yellow Hammer all have dark bronze foliage, as do bronze fennel, *Eupatorium* Chocolate, geranium Sea Spray and sedum Vera Jameson and Matrona.

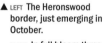
▲ LEFT **The Heronswood border, just emerging in October.**

RIGHT **In full bloom three months later, from January to March.**

Don't try for a year round peak

A garden of flowers can never look appealing for twelve months when the flowering periods of most plants are so brief. If you choose to boost your garden's appeal in winter, then the summer period will be even flatter. It is far better to concentrate on summer flowering shrubs like romneya, buddleja and lavatera, and to reduce the space given to azaleas and camellias.

The backbone of a beautiful summer garden is the planting of both perennials and annuals - particularly the group of border perennials that begins flowering in December and can remain in flower for five months, right up until the cold winter nights in May.

It wasn't until we started using the bronze-foliaged dahlias, such as Bishop of Llandaff, sedum, salvia and grasses, that we created summer borders in our gardens that would remain in flower twice as long as any English summer border. By eliminating plants that needed staking and choosing plants with beautiful foliage, we were able to create pleasing borders of contrasting foliage and harmonious flowers.

Seeing beyond the flowers

Because the flowering time of most plants is fleeting, it is the form and foliage of a plant that transforms it from the second-rate to first-rate choice for a flower garden. And so it is with a flower border. The synergy of plants creates an artistic triumph unimaginable if gardeners were to only consider obvious flowers bought on impulse.

Planning a border

Size of groups The camera is a wonderful instrument for framing beautiful pictures and exposing poor compositions and colour clashes. For a border to create a visual impact that you want to would photograph it needs to be at least 1 metre to 2 metres across at the front and a similar depth. Within a 4 metre deep bed we would arrange three to four tiers of plants with heights at the front of 30cm to 70cm, rising to 2.5 metres at the back.

Size of border Most annual or perennial borders are designed to be about twice as deep as the tallest plant. The tallest rarely reach 2.5 metres, so borders are often approximately 4 metres deep. When we grow shrubs that reach 3 metres our borders are 5 metres to 6 metres deep. Beds of more than 6 metres have so many layers of shrubs that plants are blocked from view. There is a definite limit to the area of the flower bed and this is largely determined by the scale of plants and the ease of working the bed.

Number of plants Plants should be chosen for flowers, foliage, colour and form and spaced according to their heights and width. For example, when planting penstemons, which are 60cm tall and 40cm across, they would occupy an area 0.4 metres by 0.4 metres, which equals 0.16 square metres and thereby requires six plants per square metre, or 24 plants to cover a 4 square metre area. It is impossible to create any impact with a single plant unless it reaches at least 1 metre in height, so as a general rule plant in groups of 5 to 11 plants (odd numbers look less contrived) of the shorter height. Closer spacing fills the gaps more quickly and smothers weeds but involves spending more money on plants and water.

Avoid the balcony effect

Municipal gardeners plant in rigid straight lines, creating a typical balcony effect.

While this might work for dwarf bedding plants, an artistic planting should echo nature creating triangular patterns with plants, whether they are annual or perennial.

Plant in grouped blocks of uneven size in wave-like shapes so that the foliage interweaves. Avoid unnatural circles and rectangles which are alien to nature. While tall plants are generally planted at the back they could also stand in the middle provided they didn't block the view of the background.

Maintenance of the perennial border

Perennial borders require attention throughout the year. Plant from May to August, mulch from September to October, enjoy flowers and then dead-head from December to April and cut back from May to June. Leave grasses to flower and then cut them back in September.

Annuals with perennials?

Annuals to fill gaps, such as cottage poppies and cerinthe, can be planted in the spaces created by late flowering perennials. They will flower and can be removed without disturbing the emergence of mainstay perennials.

Unfortunately annuals and perennials are rarely successful in borders together. Spring flowering perennial lupins and delphiniums tend to peak a month after spring annuals and the dying foliage of the annuals spoils the December flush of the perennials.

When planted with summer perennials that remain in the ground for twelve months, the planting and weeding of the annuals disturbs the rapidly expanding perennials.

Perennials with shrubs

The cornerstone of the summer flower garden is the planting of perennials and shrubs, particularly shrub roses. Most suburban gardeners rely on bedding annuals such as marigolds and petunias, but their lack of height, contrasting foliage and shape create a one dimensional garden with little interest compared with the subtlety and beauty of a fine border.

Creating a perennial border with evergreens and herbaceous plants, or an exclusively herbaceous border, requires great skill. Combining perennials and summer flowering shrubs is much easier.

Using a theme of grey foliage shrubs, try combining shrub roses, *Artemesia*, buddleja, *Caryopteris*, cherry pie, romneya and perennials such as catmint, coneflower and verbascum.

Summer deserves more than the
dead ends of dried up leaves.

Planting evergreen perennials – an alternative to natives

▲ Bold, spineless pads of *Opuntia* enliven hanging rosemary.

Mounding forms   LEFT **Clouds of box**   RIGHT **Santolina**

Vertical forms   LEFT *Echium wildpretii*   RIGHT *Verbascum olympicum*

Instead of a bush garden why not try evergreen perennials? Most Australian native perennials and shrubs have lower survival rates in the eastern states than plants from the Mediterranean.

Think of how tough lavender, rosemary, sage and thyme are. If you add echiums from the Canary Islands, salvia, cistus and flax, you can see there is a formidable list of plants used to 40°C heat and drought for months on end.

Many have adapted to extreme heat and drought by producing grey foliage like lavender, echium, lavender cotton and verbascum, succulent leaves and intriguing colours such as blue from *Senecio* or dark green from rosemary to survive the heat. They all have the great advantage of being outstanding foliage plants, not just for six months but even in winter (-4°C), which enables a gardener to create a rich tapestry with height, structure and colour that never looks tired after days of 40°C.

Unfortunately many Australia natives from the arid zones need poorer soils than most of our backyards offer. When they do grow well they require regular pruning and removal of dead branches. Most bush gardens that I visit have the major disadvantage of flowering in winter and spring leaving little of interest in summer and because they are survivors they create an arid, stressed look which is hardly consoling on a hot day.

I've seen stunning natural bush gardens within Cradle Mountain, the Victorian Alps and in Western Australia which put to shame any attempt at recreating the bush.

Choosing plants by shape and form

This does not mean that those who wish to plant some natives around them shouldn't but that they can widen their choices because there are far more plants that have adapted to dry, hot conditions from outside Australia than from within our coastline.

Our climate demands that we keep our thin soils covered to prevent topsoil loss.

It is therefore logical to opt for permanent plantings, not broad expanses of annual bedding plants that devour water resources, need constant weeding and after a brief gaudy display leave soils exposed. Evergreen perennials hold their foliage for twelve months.

Evergreens that tolerate dry conditions are the obvious choices. They suppress weeds and, apart from the occasional clip over and mulch, need hardly any maintenance. They are plants that revel in harsh conditions so they are less likely to be prone to pests and diseases.

There is a huge range of plants that can fit both our climate and our new mind-set; we need to look at them with new eyes. They can be moulded into a living sculpture where there is both drama and peace – even without flowers.

Foliage, form and texture should be the focus. The repetition of a simple rounded shape can be dramatic when contrasted with some strong verticals in formal gardens.

Whatever your style, start to think of shapes first rather than flowers. Imagine different sizes of rounded shapes set off by a strong vertical, add some spiky or strong upright plants, blend some low tufts and contrast with some flat mat shaped plants. Don't be seduced by visions of brilliant flowers.

The next consideration is foliage texture and colour. Consider the difference between ballota, *Euphorbia wulfenii*, rosemary and lavender. Yes, they are all roughly the same rounded shape and size, yet their colours range from rich dark green to silver and smoky grey.

Blue chalk sticks and Hen and chickens may both be the same shape (mat forming) and the same colour (silver-grey) but their textures are quite different.

Chalk sticks are a mass of vertical foliage, whereas Hen and chickens are a conglomerate of crisp rosettes. By combining and contrasting foliage colour and texture we can start to use plants as pieces that will make up a many textured and coloured sculpture.

Heronswood's evergreen border is appealing even in winter! ▲

Airy Fairy forms   LEFT Gaura   RIGHT Russian sage

 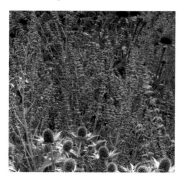

Mat forms   LEFT Hen and chickens   RIGHT Blue chalk sticks

▲ Lavender, santolina, box and green lawn – uplifting on a hot day at Killara, Portsea.

Plants of predominantly vertical shapes, be they hollyhocks at the small end of the scale, or pencil pines and Lombardy poplars at the large end, always look most effective on sloping ground because they accentuate the slope. So whether you have a garden the size of a hillside in the Mediterranean or a sloping backyard in Australia, strong vertical shapes are ideal.

However using too many strong verticals can give a hectic and hemmed impression, rather than an uplifting one – like salt, they should be used sparingly.

Conversely a preponderance of rounded shapes often seen in suburban gardens will make the garden feel heavy; like too much boring bland pasta, an unappealing stodgy mass.

Plants with no particular shape can blend the hard edges of strongly formed plants. These 'airy fairies' lend that touch of romance that no garden should be without. These 'pretties' produce airy heads of flower for months. Again they should be used with restraint as too many will feel like a formless mass of over sweet pudding.

The place for ephemerals

In gardening as in life, getting the right balance is essential. So is the new ecologically sustainable garden just planted and left?

It can be, but that would mean missing out on all the ephemeral jewels that brighten each season, such as poppies and foxgloves. A few simple wildflowers can grow amongst permanent plantings to disappear before the hot summer. They can self sow in gravel paths or pop up through loose ground covering mat-shaped plants. Hardy spring bulbs such as ixia, freesia, *Muscari* and *Ipheion* also have their place in the sun without displacing other plants.

The delicate beauty of nerines, rain lilies, *Cyclamen hederifolium* and *C. coum* brighten autumn and winter gardens. When summer is at its hottest, we can be astonished by the abrupt emergence of belladonna lilies rising triumphantly out of sunbaked soil.

Ephemeral flowers   LEFT *Verbena bonariensis*   RIGHT Muscari

Tuft forms   LEFT Burgundy pennisetum   RIGHT *Festuca glauca*

Choosing garden-worthy trees and shrubs

Australia's finest garden, the Royal Botanic Gardens Melbourne, is an outstanding garden in which to study the integration of trees and shrubs.

William Guilfoyle, who was responsible for landscaping what would become Australia's best known botanic gardens, wrote "One of the greatest essentials in landscape gardening is the variety of foliage and disposal of trees. Nothing can excel the glimpses of trees and shrubs where height and contrast of foliage have been studied.

At every step the visitor finds some new view, something fresh, lively and striking, especially when tastefully arranged. Where long, sombre rows of trees are planted and the sameness of foliage exists, the very reverse is the case."

Criteria for garden worthiness

Shrubs

1. Focus on summer for either flowering, fruiting or exceptional scent. Some (a minority) of spring or winter flowering shrubs to extend interest over 12 months.

2. Provide handsome form and foliage that integrates the house with the garden and creates cooling effect during heat waves. Avoid selections of shrubs like bottle brush with arid adapting foliage and searing red flowers.

Trees

1. Quality of shade. The worst trees – eucalypts – have leaves that hang down, letting light through to the ground. Rainforest evergreen native trees are the number one choice, with refreshing green foliage to cool the brow.

2. Ability to survive six month periods of dry soil. Deciduous trees must have drought tolerance.

3. Fits in with visual balance of the house, i.e. a suburban quarter acre block or less should have trees up to 8 metres tall, but in a large country garden, trees could be 10-30 metres tall.

4. Non-inflammability. The worst tree is the eucalyptus. The best, such as oaks or fruit trees with elegant forms, are not from fire prone areas.

In climates like the UK, where summers are cool and cloudy, arid or tropical looking plants are often chosen to create a warming effect. It's all about balancing a dominant mood – either too hot (i.e. Australian summers) or too cold (i.e. UK summers).

INSPIRING GARDENS

AUSTRALIA'S BOTANIC GARDENS

▲ Bunya pines at the Brisbane Botanic Gardens.

Herb garden at Royal Botanic Gardens, Sydney. ▼

▲ Wildflowers at Kings Park and Botanic Garden, Perth.

Lotus pond at Adelaide Botanic Garden. ▼

Planting garden-worthy shrubs and roses

▲ The foliage colour of Cloudehill's magnificent collection of trees and shrubs.

The vital first step in a garden's design is to arrange trees and shrubs as a permanent anchor to frame the house or view.

Access to the front door from the street can be given a sense of mystery by creating paths that integrate the transfer from a car dominated road into a private and peaceful garden. Straight paths are sometimes necessary in tiny front gardens but curved lines are more in keeping with the natural growth of trees and shrubs. In small gardens when the neighbours' trees not only provide privacy, but may in fact provide a feature called a borrowed landscape, then that should be incorporated into the design.

All plantings need to be sensitive to the site. Where some designers will radically alter the site's topography I firmly believe in leaving the soil profile undisturbed and using that profile to establish paths and beds around the existing space. Destroying the topsoil that has taken thousands of years to create is against all the principles of working with nature in an wholistic organic system. Most soils are deficient in carbon or minerals so there must be a good excuse to disturb soil biota.

Evergreen shrubs are the vital link between the house and the garden. By choosing foundation foliage shrubs instead of gaudy azaleas, you can lift your garden out of the ordinary. Trees and shrubs are the backbone of garden structure. Being long lived, they establish a permanence that links the house to the garden.

With their woody stems and deeper roots, shrubs survive water stress better than the shorter, shallower-rooted perennials and annuals. They are the vital skeleton around which decorative flower planting and recreational lawns are established.

Shrubs, including roses, usually have multiple trunks which distinguishes them from trees. Some, such as lavender, grow less than one metre and are called sub-shrubs, while others such as buddlejas can be ten metres tall. Australian gardens have a much longer growing season than most northern hemisphere gardens. Heat stress and water shortages can limit our choice of shrubs. To strengthen gardens we need to select far more drought-tolerant evergreens, such as wigandia and honey bush, in place of the water-demanding deciduous shrubs such as magnolia and hydrangea.

Foundation shrubs

The highly admired American Foundation planting was a device used to block from view the foundations of the house. Today it defines a style in which shrubs are chosen for their foliage and form to harmonise with their associated buildings.

Unfortunately, Australian gardeners and nursery owners have chosen obvious one-dimensional shrubs that seek attention with short lived large flowers rather than provide a solid landscape link to the house. The eye needs rest from excessive stimulation. Gardens suffer when we choose shrubs for flowers alone, such as fuchsia, hybrid tea rose, hibiscus and bougainvillea.

Roses need companions

For the last 2,000 years the plant that nearly every person in every country in the world has preferred above all others is the rose. So distracted and helplessly in love are some rose fanatics that they are completely blinded by its numerous faults.

It goes without saying that the rose in bud, like a freshly opened tulip, is perfection, particularly when set in a vase in pride of place inside. Few other flowers have the fragrance that causes women to swoon as if hopelessly in love. But these two epic attractions are rarely useful when creating beautiful pictures outside the house.

LEFT Albertine has ▲ extravagant, all-at-once flowering.

CENTRE A rose garden needs structure so climbing roses transform a normally shapeless plant.

RIGHT Roses look best with companions such as clematis.

For four months in winter the stems, bereft of leaves and covered in spines, are ugly and unfriendly. In spring the modern floribundas and hybrid teas leave unfilled, spindly stems that need cover with companions and the leaves are flat, dull and create a monotonous, visually boring picture mostly disturbed (in many gardens) by ghastly colour clashes when the masses of blooms burst.

Shrub roses – old roses revisited

While most modern rose breeders concentrated on commercial cut flower hybrid tea cultivars and floribundas rather than garden roses, David Austin began the process of improving the performance of roses for garden display. By combining the health, vigour and repeat flowering of modern roses with the fragrance of Damasks and complex open buds, a reinvigorated, beautiful shrub evolved in every colour with the unexpected benefit of suiting Australia's hot summers better than in England where they were created.

Choose shrubs for form and foliage

To strengthen gardens during summer, which is when we use them most, choose shrubs with foliage, form and flowers. Lavender is a classic example. Its grey foliage contrasts wonderfully with the green of other shrubs and its flowers are only a secondary element in the picture it creates. Far too many of the shrubs we plant are quite ordinary-looking plants once their flowers have disappeared.

There are many wonderful evergreen shrubs with dark green foliage, such as rosemary, box, *Murraya*, myrtle and gardenia, which provide solidity and also have subtle, but charming flowers. Rose flowers may be showy, but it is impossible to create lovely pictures with roses alone. Beautiful gardens can be created when roses are the secondary feature, using evergreen shrubs and perennials to balance the picture.

Combine roses with annuals and perennials

Most gardeners have a favourite rose flower colour scheme. Pink is the easiest colour to work with, while red is the most difficult. By planting blue or purple annuals and perennials that harmonise with roses an ordinary rose garden will be transformed. In a pink rose garden use spring flowering blue annuals such as blue lace flower, Canterbury bells, cornflowers, forget-me-nots and love-in-a-mist.

Appropriate spring flowering blue perennials include campanula, catmint and columbines. Summer flowering blue perennials for a pink rose garden include ageratum, *Aster frikartii*, catmint, delphinium Blue Sensation, *Eryngium*, Electric Blue penstemon and Russian sage.

Spring flowering purple annuals that would suit a pink rose garden include Californian poppy, cerinthe, foxglove and peony poppy. Appropriate spring flowering purple perennials include columbine and wallflower, while suitable summer flowering purple perennials include coneflower, penstemon Midnight, salvia Purple Rain and *Trachelium*.

Shrubs to be enjoyed for their fragrance

Fragrance need not be sacrificed for foliage as many shrubs contribute both to a garden. Among these are *Azara*, buddleja, *Cestrum*, daphne, gardenia, cherry pie, lavender, lilac, *Luculia*, *Murraya*, *Osmanthus*, *Philadelphus*, wintersweet and *Viburnum*.

Shrubs whose actual foliage is aromatic include *Caryopteris*, *Cistus*, curry plant, cushion bush, lavender, pelargonium, *Prostanthera*, rosemary, cotton lavender, *Vitex* and wormwood.

These hybrid tea roses in a vase show that mixed ▲ colours such as pink, red, white and yellow roses in a single eye frame are discordant. If a green background separated the colours, each colour on its own would be more appealing.

Ephemeral fillers – bulbs

▲ Naturalised bulbs at St Erth.

Bulbs are like a soufflé, providing delicious seasonal highlights but never the main course.

Bulbs are precious jewels of flowers: they are impressive and hugely decorative, but they are the ephemera of the flowering world, most appearing for no more than two weeks a year. The famous carpets of colour that attract millions of visitors to Keukenhof in the Netherlands every spring are quite bare after flowering and for the rest of the year.

Bulbs are best planted with other companions and not alone in their own feature beds. Bulbs flower so briefly that a garden planted with bulbs alone can be a huge disappointment.

Mature gardeners learn to raise bulbs as the entree or dessert and organise the main course around shrubs and perennials which provide the year round form and structure. All bulbs have swollen storage organs enabling them to survive until conditions are suitable for growth.

To adapt to harsh seasonal conditions in their natural habitat many retreat below the ground. Dormancy is brought on by winter cold, as is the case with dahlias, or summer drought as with tulips and daffodils.

In more favourable climates with summer moisture and mild winters, bulbs like clivia and agapanthus retain their leaves and are true evergreens.

The term 'bulb' includes tubers like dahlias, rhizomes such as bearded iris and corms like gladioli. These are the easiest of plants to cultivate because the flowers are already formed in the bulb and they multiply without attention in well-drained, sunny conditions. The planting depth is about two to three times as deep as the bulb width.

Most of the spring flowering bulbs that thrive in Australia come from the sunny Mediterranean or South Africa where they enjoy wet winters, warm to hot springs and dry, hot summers. These bulbs do poorly in Sydney and Brisbane if summers are wet as this stimulates growth when the bulbs need to rest.

The most beautiful bulb, the exquisite tulip, is best regarded as an annual and replanted each year, as 90 per cent of Australia is not cold enough for it to survive a second season.

Even artificial cooling in a refrigerator at 5°C for eight weeks can be insufficient to initiate flowering and the buds often abort. If planted deeper, where the soil temperature is cooler, tulips will naturalise, but if the buds emerge when spring temperatures rise above 24°C the flowering display will be brief.

Bulbs with shrubs or naturalised in grass

Many gardeners prefer to grow daffodils. These are reliable, appearing year after year and easily naturalise under fruit trees or on sunny plains, provided the foliage is allowed to die naturally to nurture the creation of next year's flower.

Most of our favourite bulbs, such as bluebells, daffodils, *Ipheion*, *Ixia*, *Lachanalia*, *Muscari*, snowflake, *Sparaxis* and *Tritonia* naturalise beautifully in informal beds in front of shrubs or in grassy areas that can be left completely unattended.

Many of our most treasured bulbs that have been bred especially for sale as florist flowers are best planted in separate areas where their removal doesn't weaken garden structure. These include hyacinth, hybrid freesias, tulips and gladioli.

CREATING BEAUTY
Ephemeral fillers – heirloom annuals and biennials

The greatest weakness in using annuals is that no matter how exuberant and willing they are to flower, very few have form or foliage that compare with those of evergreen structural plants in a flower garden.

Annuals are largely decorative, the dessert element of a three-course meal and never the main course. But argemone, Californian poppy, cerinthe, celosia, cottage poppies and hunnemannias have good grey foliage. Amaranth, celosias and coleus have good purple foliage and variegated honesty and snow-on-the-mountain have good white foliage tints.

Taking care with colour

Because annuals are the showiest of flowers, they must be treated with the greatest care. A garden that displays the full spectrum of colours is gaudy, tiring and an assault on our visual sense. *Bedding plants sold in a full range of mixed colours are always to be avoided.* Although colour is a matter of personal taste it is much safer to separate colours into three groups: pastels, hot colours like red and yellow, and white. Colour intensity depends on whether flowers are double or single; cottage gardeners invariably choose single flowers while modern suburban gardeners prefer larger double flowers.

Where to grow annuals

Incongruously the showiest of flowers are those that are out of flower the longest (or so it seems, because they leave the gaps in a garden for the greatest length of time). Annuals are grown in the spring cottage garden and then the summer cottage garden in their own dedicated areas rather than combined with perennials or shrubs.

Although they are the least structural of plants and would benefit from the foliage and form of perennial neighbours, they have to be planted and removed at a time that disturbs the maintenance of perennials. Bedding annuals always look best against a formal box hedge because the hedge holds the garden together when the annuals are out of flower.

Biennials are all hardy plants that must grow through a cold winter to stimulate flowering in spring before they set seed and die in summer.

Cerinthe is a more subtle ▲ hardy annual with grey foliage that fits in with other plants.

The cycle often takes up to eighteen months depending on sowing time. Foxgloves are the most popular biennial. If not planted in the garden early enough in winter they will disappoint by merely sitting there taking up valuable space for a further twelve months before flowering the following spring.

Hardy and tender

HARDY ANNUALS are those that will survive a frost. They come from the cooler parts of the world where their seeds naturally fall into the soil to sit through winter, then begin to emerge when soil temperatures rise to between 10°C and 12°C. Best sown in February and March and planted out in late April and May, almost all will flower in spring rather than summer and so become the backbone of a spring garden. If planted as late as early spring they will still flower before Christmas.

TENDER ANNUALS all come from warm temperate, sub-tropical and tropical areas where frost is unknown. They drop their seeds and because the soil temperatures are invariably over 20°C the seeds germinate readily. If planted in areas with cold winters these plants will be cut down by frost. If they are to survive they must be raised like tomatoes - protected from frost for eight weeks and planted out when soil temperature is above 20°C.

They can be sown as late as December in areas where the growing season is at least ninety days longer than the usual flowering period. For example, cosmos begin flowering in about 80 days and continue for another 90 days. They could be late-sown anywhere that the growing season exceeds 170 days.

Step-by-step sowing

▲ LEFT **Exquisite poppies to swap seeds with like-minded gardeners.**

RIGHT **'S' patterns are preferred for direct sown seed of wildflowers, so there are no unnaturally created straight lines.**

Outdoors

1 Effective weed control is absolutely essential to the success of any planting. Don't sow in straight rows, which are alien to nature, but in sweeping 'S' shapes (as shown above) at least 10 to 20cm apart so that you can till easily between the 'S' shapes. When mature flowers join up and gaps are eliminated, the overall patterns look more natural. Lay down newspapers or weed mats to block light from emerging weeds and cover it with a fine layer of weed-free soil (2cm only). Seedling roots break through the paper readily.

2 Sow in late autumn or early spring, after effective weed control. Wildflower areas re-germinate naturally in early April and late August, when soil temperatures are about 12°C. At this time moisture levels are high and sowings probably won't need supplementary watering. Sowings as late as October or November will require daily waterings.

3 A fine tilth will ensure that soil and seed make contact. The growing of wildflowers is no more difficult than sowing vegetable seeds at home or, on a large scale, the growing of wheat. A well prepared, weed free, friable soil ensures successful establishment.

4 Many wildflower seeds are as fine as table salt, making them difficult to sow evenly. Mix seed with dry sand using an amount of sand two to five times the weight of the seeds to distribute the seeds more easily. Most packets of seeds specify areas to be covered, but if not, sow approximately 850 seeds per square metre, or seventy-five seeds per square foot. Denser sowings produce weak, spindly seedlings, while lighter sowings may not provide adequate cover.

5 After annuals flower and set seed, cut plants to the ground with a whipper snipper. If seeds re-emerge in late autumn without weeds, a resowing will not be needed for a spring display. If weeds appear, weed the area and resow in late autumn or early spring.

6 Annuals begin flowering in eight to sixteen weeks. Water and weed as required.

Indoors

This method is most effective for very fine seeds or tender annuals that need warmer temperatures to sprout in areas with a short growing season. Choose a warm, well-lit spot: spindly seedlings are a result of too little light.

1 Fill the punnet with seedling soil mix to within 1cm of the top.

2 Firm with a woodblock.

3 Water gently but thoroughly.

4 Sow the seed on top, hardy seeds at 10°C to 12°C and tender ones at 15°C to 20°C.

5 Sieve some seedling mix over the seeds to a depth of two to three times the seeds' width.

6 Water in lightly. Seedlings usually emerge in fourteen to twenty days and can be pricked out into individual pots when they have developed their second set of leaves (not the 'seed leaves' - their first 'true leaves').

If transplanting into the garden, wait until they have three sets of leaves or more, depending upon the space in the punnet. Overcrowded seedlings become diseased.

Sowing wildflowers

Annuals are the most prolific flowering plants in the botanic world.

Although only one seed is needed for the plant to reproduce, some, like the peony poppy, produce up to 100,000 seeds per plant. Almost all annuals are easy to raise from seed and most germinate in fourteen days. Annuals require open soil that must be cultivated and this encourages weeds to germinate. The battle for supremacy in the seed bed is often lost if weeds aren't decapitated with a Dutch hoe weeks after germination.

Most professional seed merchants sow annuals directly into the soil and Dutch hoe the weeds at four and eight weeks, when they are easy to control. Instead of raising seedlings or buying transplanted seedlings, gardeners should save time and money by starting their annual flower borders from a direct sowing.

After flowering be sure to deadhead the mature seed pods, because prolific seed producers like poppies can drop millions of seeds that you may not want next year (a weed is a plant growing in the wrong place!).

A wildflower garden of annuals

Many gardeners are returning to the growing of annual wildflowers. These follow the rhythms of nature, being sown after autumn rains, germinating and growing through the cool months and flowering in late spring before soils dry out. They grow readily from seed and will resow after flowering if happy, so they require a minimal amount of effort.

Wildflowers are the source of our cultivated flowers and originally were found on the prairies of America, in the cornfields of Europe and on the plains of southern Africa, California and Australia.

It's the least amount of work!

The amount of work required for a wildflower garden is just a fraction of the amount required to plant annual seedlings because you don't have the tedious job of planting out seedlings and then watering them. It takes only about ten minutes to sow and rake in the seeds for a wildflower garden (less than a quarter of the time required to plant out seedlings), and there are hardly any weeds.

TOP **Ladybird poppies.** ▲
BOTTOM **Native everlasting.**

How much seed do I need?

Measure the area to be sown. A 100 square metre area is ten paces by ten paces, or five paces by twenty paces. A hectare of annuals is 100 metres by 100 metres, or 10,000 square metres, and just as easy to sow as a hectare of wheat!

Flanders poppy contains an incredible 7,000 seeds per gram, so a gram of seed, costing $3.50, is enough to cover almost 10 square metres. If you covered the same area with spring daffodils, it would cost about $5,000.

Wildflowers thrive in uncultivated, poor soil supplied by natural rainfall and there is no need to buy fertiliser.

CREATING BEAUTY

WITH EDIBLES

Creating beauty with vegetables

A plan for an ornamental edible garden

My interest in gardening developed from the very first time I walked around Melbourne's botanic garden.

I was fascinated by its beauty and its complexity but above all, it was its use of plants expressed creatively. So it was the aesthetics of gardening that was always of greater interest to me than the simple practicalities of growing. Later, after having travelled through the finest country gardens in England and studying the gardens of Hidcote and Sissinghurst, I was impatient to create my own.

To learn about art by planting

Whilst the permaculture movement was gaining popularity at that time I was perpetually irritated by the inability of its leaders to acknowledge that gardening is an art form which need not be sacrificed in the pursuit of sustainable systems of food production.

Gardening is a visual art form

How many times must we blink our eyes to avoid looking at the recycled water bottles, the white foam boxes, the recycled, corrugated iron, raised beds that enclose pots of vegetables? *Is there an unspoken permaculture rule which states that it is frivolous to make productive gardens beautiful?* Fortunately it costs no more to grow vegetables, fruit and herbs in beautiful surroundings than it does when we just grow food for the table.

In the Loire Valley, near the famous Chateau Villandry, is a garden that has a festival each year to allow poets, painters, sculptors and gardeners to express their art in the outdoors. Unlike the Chelsea Flower Show, Chaumont's festival is about art outdoors and plants are just one of the visual art forms.

At Heronswood we have five food gardens, each designed to appeal to our senses, including our parterre, our herb gardens, our kitchen garden and our food borders. We continually strive to integrate our food plants within our garden plans by eliminating straggly branched fruit such as plums and replacing those trees with pomegranates and persimmons, olives and custard apples.

Surely there is "no excuse for ugliness as beauty properly understood is cheap". EDWARD LA TROBE BATEMAN, circa 1860s

With vegetables

▲ Vegetable beds at
Chateau Villandry,
France.

A potager in a parterre

Just as the English developed the
decorative flower garden and its finest
expression in the cottage garden,
it was the French who created the
supreme triumph of art over craft in the
wonderful vegetable garden at Villandry.

Villandry is the culmination of two very strong
French traditions; their great love of food and
elegance, expressed in strict geometric patterns –
le potager en parterre.

Instead of planting in rows, a series of interesting
symmetrical patterns are edged with the dark
toning of English box and separated by the light
beige gravel paths.

▼ FROM LEFT TO RIGHT
Nasturtium Alaska,
artichoke Italian Purple,
Five Colour silverbeet,
Scarlet Runner bean and
Red Drumhead cabbage.

Within each parterre are sumptuous groupings
of vegetables with interesting foliage so that
the effect, when viewed from above, is of a rich
embroidered tapestry.

Creating beauty with vegetables

Rather than attempt to copy Villandry, at
Heronswood we decided to create a vegetable
garden using our natural turf for paths and its
sharp edges to describe the patterns we wanted to
express. The cut turf gives almost instant results
(just a few weekends digging) and saves all the
expense and waiting until the box is large enough
to define the pattern. *A parterre a l'Australien!*

We settled on a circular design with six segments
of sixty degrees bisected by six paths to enable us
to sow, hoe and harvest easily. This layout also
suits crop rotations, where nitrogen-producing
legume crops are followed by leaf crops (heavy
feeders) – rotating the crops at each planting
helps prevent the buildup of soil diseases.

The planting beds had been covered by densely
thatched turf so we had no weed seeds to bring
to the surface when we first dug it over and
planted the seeds. When it comes to planting
the vegetables, the secret of success is to arrange
vegetables into three groupings, keeping the
untidy sprawling kinds like pumpkins out of the
cut turf parterre and relegated behind (or up) a
two metre trellis, out of sight.

Up this trellis, at both ends, we grow soil building
legumes such as beans in summer and peas and
sweet peas in winter. Within the two metre
apron in front of the trellis, we plant the less tidy
and taller growing vegetables such as sweet corn,
silverbeet and tomatoes.

It's surprising how many vegetables have
interestingly coloured leaves and fruits, such
as the rich, bold colours of Tuscan black kale
or the changing reds and yellows of five colour
silverbeet. When the predominant background
colour is green from the grassy paths the grey
foliage of leeks and the blue leaves of the red
cabbage become fascinating highlights.

The feathery tops of carrots are interesting next to the rounded shapes of lettuce and the deep green crinkle-cut leaves of January King cabbage. There are lots of fun, contrasting colours, such as yellow pansies or the dwarf marbled leaves of nasturtium Alaska with blue cabbages.

Black pansy combines beautifully with the grey upright stems of leeks and all the lettuces make a fascinating checkerboard when grown with brown freckles lettuce, green-heading lettuces and Italian Red chicory.

If you don't wish to plant a second crop of vegetables after the first harvest in autumn, then use your parterre as a flower garden. It would be a great success with all the 'already dwarfed' bedding plants such as pansies, primulas, English daisies, dwarf sweet peas and Iceland poppies, whose flowering would be finished in November ready for summer planting.

In summer try mixing up red salvias with parsley, nasturtium Alaska, with its marbled foliage, and petunias or dwarf zinnias.

The design also lends itself to the planting of a herb garden using the greys of lavender and cotton lavender to offset parsley, sage, rosemary and thyme. These herbs could easily fit into a mixed planting of vegetables and flowers each spring or autumn.

Around the outer circle of our cut turf parterre we planted a lemon tree and grapefruit tree because they are evergreen. The fruits are interesting in winter, but kumquats or oranges could also be used.

For those wishing to plant more fruit, citrus trees could be used to provide an evergreen edible screen or dwarf fruit could be espaliered to increase fruit production. Our only maintenance, other then normal cultivation, is to trim the turf edges and to cut the hedge twice a year.

Planting vegetables in patterns instead of rows requires careful grading of heights and colours but the final result will look just as appealing as our finest flower gardens.

TOP **A spring parterre** ▶
CENTRE **Using cabbages and nasturtiums as highlights.**
BOTTOM **A winter parterre.**

A plan for an ornamental edible garden

Deciduous fruiting shade trees

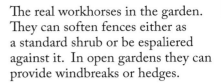

What miraculous things. They supply winter sun, summer shade, autumn foliage and often spring blossom plus their luscious fruit. They certainly outperform the ornamental flowering cherries and plums that are so ubiquitous.

In hot climates they can shelter summer potatoes, lettuces or pumpkins and in winter allow enough light through to raise broccoli, cabbages and beetroot. Deciduous trees allow gardeners to vary their microclimates with the season.

Small varieties Almond, *apricot, *fig, quince, persimmon, pistachio, medlar, *plum, *mulberry, *pear, apple, *cherry, Chinese date, *nectarine and *peach.

* *Best not to plant near paths or paving as the fallen fruit can be messy – or eat the fruit before it drops!*

Large varieties Walnut, chestnut and pecan.

Evergreen shade trees

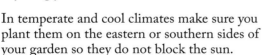

A boon in hot climates. Not only do they provide year-round shade, they can screen the next door neighbours and generally blot out anything you don't want to look at.

In temperate and cool climates make sure you plant them on the eastern or southern sides of your garden so they do not block the sun.

Varieties Avocado, mango, custard apple, olive, loquat, white sapote, macadamia, carob and citrus on citrange rootstock.

Plants that attract beneficial insects

 Pollinator   Predator

Bergamot, borage, catmint, daisy family, daffodil/jonquil, dill, fennel, gaura, lavender, lemon balm, mint, onion family, oregano/ marjoram, parsley family, poppies, rosemary, salvia, germander and thyme.

Evergreen shrubs and hedges

The real workhorses in the garden. They can soften fences either as a standard shrub or be espaliered against it. In open gardens they can provide windbreaks or hedges.

You will never have to plant the ultra-boring pittosporum again. Small evergreen shrubs can be used to edge the garden beds or use them in drifts in front of larger plants as others might plant azalea or diosma.

Varieties to 1.5m Lavender, rosemary, *Naranjilla*, natal plum, shrubby salvias, marguerite daisy, Chilean guava and citrus on dwarf rootstock.

Varieties to 3m Avocado, *carob, bay tree, *pineapple guava*, olive, *strawberry guava and citrus on citrange rootstock.

* *Also make good windbreaks.*

Deciduous shrubs and hedges

These chameleons provide shade in summer and allow light in winter. Many deciduous fruit trees on dwarfing rootstocks function more like shrubs in the garden and, when espaliered, form permeable hedges that allow glimpses of the garden beyond without revealing all. Grow flowering plants that supply food for beneficial insects or spread a mat of alpine or forest strawberries underneath. Prickly 'shrubs' and hedges like berries and roses also make great habitat for native birds.

Varieties to 1.5m Raspberries, currants, gooseberry, lemon verbena, bronze fennel, *Chaenomeles* and roses that produce hips with single flowers (e.g. *Rosa rugosa*).

Varieties to 3m Pomegranate, hazel, blueberry and large, trellised cane berries (e.g. loganberries, boysenberries etc.).

Accent plants

These plants usually have strongly vertical foliage to contrast with the more usual rounded shapes in the garden. The contrast works in the same way as combining lemon and sugar. Two very different elements working each to enhance the other.

Large varieties jelly palm, babaco, banana and paw paw.

Small varieties kale, leeks, pineapple, silverbeet, lemon grass and globe artichoke.

Garden beds – vegetable beds

Vegetables, being largely annuals and biennials, are short-lived plants so garden beds can be dug over and changed at will. The shape of garden beds may be important to the long-term structure of a garden but their content can vary with the seasons. Traditional annual bedding plants like petunias are easily replaced in the food garden with lettuces, cabbage and nasturtium.

Plant perennials near trees and shrub, as they do not have to be removed every few months; they do not disturb the roots of permanent plantings. Plant asparagus, rhubarb, strawberries, and herbs with some smaller shrubs.

Ground covers/pots strawberries, alyssum, ground cherry, nasturtiums, cranberries, pepino, vegetables and herbs.

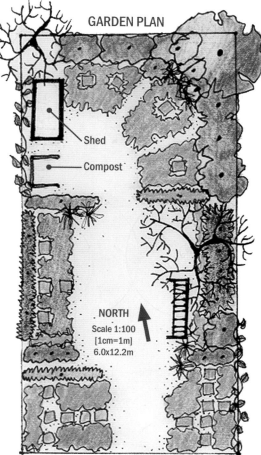

GARDEN PLAN

Shed

Compost

NORTH
Scale 1:100
[1cm=1m]
6.0x12.2m

▲ TOP PLAN
Shade in summer is 25%.
30% lawn and 45% beds.

BOTTOM PLAN ▼
Shade in summer is 20%
15% lawn and 65% beds.

Legend

Evergreen Shade

Deciduous Shade

Evergreen Shrub

Espaliered Deciduous

Evergreen Hedge

Cane Berries

Espaliered Evergreen

Berry Bushes

Garden Beds

Accent Plants

Strawberries

Climbers

Pots

Lawn

Stepping Stones

Bench

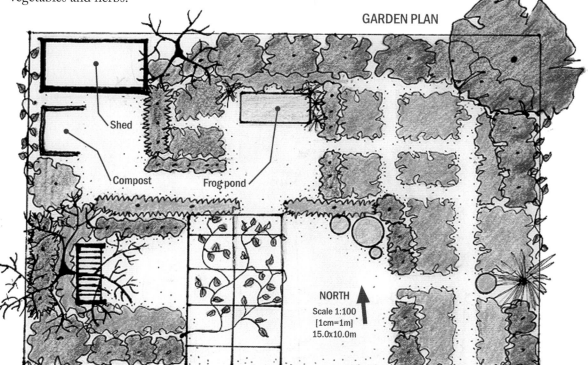

GARDEN PLAN

Shed

Compost

Frog pond

NORTH
Scale 1:100
[1cm=1m]
15.0x10.0m

HERB GARDENS

HERONSWOOD

CREATING BEAUTY
Evergreen herb gardens

The word 'herb' is synonymous with herbaceous foliage which includes annuals, perennials and bulbs but strictly not plants with woody stems such as trees and shrubs.

In the years before the development of science, herbs were grown medicinally to cure ailments and herb gardens became vitally important scientific gardens developed within church monastries because this was the centre of knowledge, housing all the published books stacked in their libraries.

Today we usually grow annuals in a vegetable or flower garden, rely on pharmaceuticals as medicines and place perennial flowers in specific borders as we do at Heronswood, St Erth or Cloudehill.

So the modern herb garden is an echo of past needs. It has a place today because it will usually include all the fresh culinary herbs in a small garden enclosure that suits inner city spaces.

By widening its original definition to include Mediterranean trees and shrubs such as bay tree, rosemary and lavender it survives because it is a pleasing contemplative space based upon evergreen planting that looks appealing for twelve months of the year.

The creation of an appealing herb garden requires the use of perennial herbs with good foliage and form – see our **HERB SELECTOR** on pages 64-65.

HERB KNOT GARDEN, BARNSLEY, UK

Rosemary

Moroccan Mint

Spanish Lavender

Sage

Thyme

Oregano Thumble's Gold

Golden Marjoram

Allium nutans

Apple Mint

HERB GARDEN, SISSINGHURST, UK

Dill ANNUAL

Parsley BIENNIAL

Sweet Mace

Chervil ANNUAL

Vietnamese Mint

Sweet Basil ANNUAL

Lawn Chamomile

Chives

Coriander ANNUAL

BASIC BOTANY

Basic botany for gardening success
by Bill Bampton, head gardener at Heronswood

The sun – the source of plant energy

The carbon cycle

The soil – living, breathing and feeding plants

Nutrition – feed the soil, not the plants

Composting – making soils and mulches

Pests and diseases

Plant forms and life cycle

Temperature – choosing the right plants

Dozo – Heronswood's ▲
resident garden gnome.

The sun – the source of plant energy

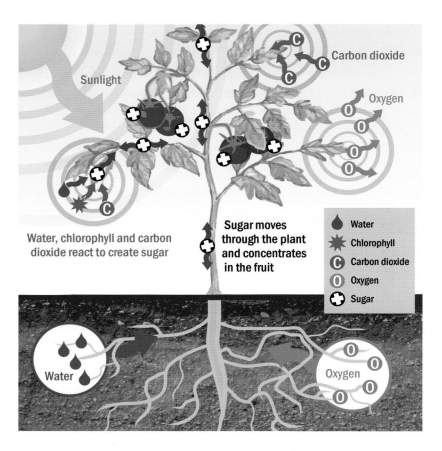

Sunlight

Carbon dioxide

Oxygen

Water, chlorophyll and carbon dioxide react to create sugar

Sugar moves through the plant and concentrates in the fruit

Water

Oxygen

- ● Water
- ✳ Chlorophyll
- Ⓒ Carbon dioxide
- Ⓞ Oxygen
- ✚ Sugar

One of the most profound mistakes we can make as gardeners is to overrate our importance and ability to control our garden.

We have a vision of how we want our garden to be: bountiful, lush, and blossoming. We read garden books, learn a list of rules, symptoms, cures and pests, we visit the garden centre and return with the appropriate pesticides and chemical fertilisers as recommended by the expert or product label.

Yet, still we get those spots on the rose leaf. We are on an endless cycle using more and more inputs and precious water and still our imagined garden eludes us. The truth is the inhabitants of our gardens, the plants, soil, birds and animals are oblivious to our aspiration; they are too busy getting on with their own lives. A truly successful organic garden is *"a place where we can meet nature halfway"* (Michael Pollan). We can do this by improving our understanding of the lives of the plants we tend and the environment they grow in.

This does not mean we need a degree in ecology, it does mean we need to know about the areas where our desires as gardeners to feed ourselves and to create beauty meet with the drives and desires of the plants we tend.

We need to go beyond rote learnt rules and recipes and look at the underlying biology of gardening. This is the first of a series of articles looking at some of the basic "hows" and "whys" of gardening, beginning with the very basics of how plants feed themselves.

Photosynthesis and chlorophyll

Photosynthesis is the engine of the food we eat and the oxygen we breathe. Yet it is only partially understood and while the process itself has been around since the beginning of life, the awkward word used to describe it has only been around since 1893. I think we have all been exposed to a lesson on photosynthesis dense with terminology, equations and something called the Calvin Cycle.

As gardeners we need not get bogged down in the intricacies of the process, but we do need to understand some of its implications for plant growth.

Indeed the majority of our successes and failures with plants can relate to how photosynthesis has either been inhibited or promoted. Photosynthesis is the process by which plants harness the energy of light to create sugars from water and carbon dioxide (CO_2), producing oxygen (O_2) as a by-product.

This takes place in the chlorophyll found in the green parts of plants. Plants absorb water through their roots and carbon dioxide through the pores (or stomata) in their leaves. Leaf structure facilitates the absorption of gases from the atmosphere, they are permeable and their shape maximises surface area.

Reactions in the chlorophyll convert light energy into chemical energy in the form of sugars. The sugars produced are either used in respiration or stored as starch.

This storage of excess for the future is why we should avoid the temptation to cut off foliage from bulbs once flowering is past; they are still producing food for next year's flowering.

These sugars are building blocks for many other plant compounds such as: cellulose, lignin, proteins, vitamins, hormones and enzymes. Sugars travel through the plant concentrating in shoot and root tips, here growth is fastest. Vegetable gardeners should take note: shoots, tips and fast growth are sweet to eat.

For the gardener the most important thing to understand about photosynthesis is its limiting factors. The range of light intensity for optimum photosynthesis for a plant usually relates to the microclimate in which it evolved.

Plants from prairie or desert conditions function and flower best in full sun, plants of the forest floor suiting shade or indoor situations. This relates to the position we place a plant: *Clivia robusta* from the forested swamps of Pondoland, South Africa in full shade, *Salvia chamaedryoides* from the Sierra Madre Oriental Deserts of Mexico, full sun.

The clivia has large strappy green leaves maximising access to limited light. The salvia has small grey leaves; it is more concerned with sunburn and water loss than maximising light for photosynthesis. If plants are exposed to light levels beyond their level of tolerance cells are damaged, "burnt" by high levels of ultra violet light.

Light and temperature

Photosynthesis can only occur in a temperature range from 0 to about 50 degrees Celsius. Again plants range of tolerances varies according to their origins.

Lowland tropical plants obviously have higher temperature requirements than alpine temperate plants. A general optimum temperature is between 20 and 30 degrees Celsius. As we continue to get more days of extreme temperature in the upper thirties and forties we will experience more plants, especially those evolved in cool temperate zones, displaying heat stress.

Gardeners often mistake this for lack of water. For example, many plants from the cool temperate forests of New Zealand survived years of drought conditions in Australia but succumbed dramatically to days of extended heat in the high 30s.

How light intensity ▲
conditions leaf form:

TOP Tiny grey salvia leaves indicate intense light.

MIDDLE Golden leaves indicate semi-shade conditions.

BOTTOM Large, strap-like clivia leaves indicate low light.

In the garden, temperature is one of the limiting factors hardest to control except through plant selection. Just as plants respond to fluctuations in light so too many plants respond to changes in temperature – unsurprisingly, this is called thermoperiodism.

This can often be linked to day length. The classic example of this is the chill requirements of fruits like cherries or the onset of autumn leaf colour.

While only a small amount of water is required for the actual reactions of photosynthesis, the limiting effect of water comes into play as stomata close to conserve water loss and so limit the entry of carbon dioxide. Water is also vital in maintaining the transportation of essential minerals from roots to leaves.

Light and photoperiodism

In addition to fuelling photosynthesis the other key effect of light on plants is to govern their daily and seasonal cycles, a process called 'photoperiodism'.

Photoperiodism is a plants response to the timing of light and darkness during the daily cycle. Using a light sensitive pigment called phytochrome plants actually 'measure' the length of darkness and light. It effects plant growth, seed germination, flowering, fruit development bulb formation and dormancy.

So it is often crucial if we want a plant to fruit, flower or form a bulb we need to know the duration of light/darkness it requires.

Plants have different responses to the relative length of days and nights. Some can be very specific. So, just as you can divide plants according to the intensity of light they require, shade or full sun, you can also divide them according to duration.

Short-Day plants commence flowering or bulb set when days are shorter and nights longer; Long-Day plants obviously are triggered by lengthening days shortening nights. For instance, garlic planted in autumn grows over winter but only forms cloves as the nights shorten and days lengthen in spring/summer.

Different varieties have different trigger points so you can extend the garlic season by planting late and early varieties. The same is true of sweet pea varieties. At other times you may choose to grow Long-Day plants in short day conditions to avoid flowering or bolting particularly with leaf vegetables.

For the gardener understanding the plants requirements of light duration can be as important as understanding if it is shade tolerant or sun loving.

Short-Day plants

Short-Day plants commence flowering or bulb set when days are shorter and nights longer. Garlic and onion bulbs form after the shortest day of the year and heirloom strawberries initiate fruiting.

Long-Day plants

Long Day plants are triggered by lengthening days shortening nights. Dahlias, sedums and Long-Day sweet peas need long summer days to flower.

Day neutral plants

Plants that flower and fruit regardless of day length including roses, tomatoes, corn and cucumber.

C4 plants absorb CO_2 in the dark

Some plants use additional photosynthetic pathways to the general form of photosynthesis (C3), these are CAM and C4 plants adapted to drought and high temperatures. CAM plants are able to absorb carbon dioxide at night with their stomata closed during the heat of the day. C4 plants are "faster" at absorbing carbon dioxide allowing them to out-compete other plants when conditions of temperature and water are limiting.

As gardeners we can use this knowledge to guide our plant selection. A good example is when choosing turf grasses for hot dry conditions. Throughout Australia we have seen the replacement of drought sensitive C3 grasses like ryegrass with heat and drought tolerant C4 grasses like kikuyu and buffalo or native kangaroo grass. Those that believe in the powers of GM are currently involved in the C4 rice project that seeks to transform rice, naturally a C3 grass, into a warm season C4 crop.

There are very low levels of carbon dioxide in the atmosphere; about 0.035%. Increasing carbon dioxide can increase the rate of photosynthesis.

In the vast glasshouses of industrial tomato production not only temperature and light are controlled, even carbon dioxide levels are raised to 0.1-0.15%.

In the home garden the only lift in carbon dioxide is likely to come as a result of human induced climate change. By going back to some of the basic requirements of plants I hope to encourage you to look at your garden and its plants – are you fulfilling their needs?

Look at where the light falls in your garden, you can use the light metre on your camera if it helps. Then look at the type of plants you are growing there, are their light requirements met? Do a bit of research.

What microclimate did they evolve in? Look at the timing of your vegetable plantings; did I plant my garlic late? Is this why there is still only one clove?!

The carbon cycle

The plants of the world are the great regulators of CO_2 in the atmosphere. They consume CO_2 to produce their food in photosynthesis releasing oxygen.

Conversely, as they consume their food through respiration they use oxygen and release CO_2 back into the atmosphere. This maintains a rough equilibrium, along the way humans and other animals also consume some of the oxygen and release CO_2 as we breathe.

Carbon is stored in the earth, the oceans and in everything that has ever lived, including fossil fuels. Through clearing vegetation for agriculture, tilling soil and burning fossil fuels for industry humans have dramatically increased the CO_2 levels in the atmosphere.

Carbon dioxide is a greenhouse gas, it traps solar radiation so plays a role in regulating the planets temperatures. An increase in greenhouse gases is leading to global warming, resulting higher temperatures and more extreme unpredictable weather.

As gardeners we can do our bit to help reverse the flow of carbon into the atmosphere:

- Plant the biggest tree we can within our garden.

- If we have an existing large tree, cherish it (even if its roots or leaves might give us grief occasionally).

- Stop using pesticides and fertilisers that require large amounts of fossil fuels to manufacture.

- Incorporate organic matter (carbon) in our soil.

- Grow our own organic food.

- Buy locally produced food, limiting transport emissions.

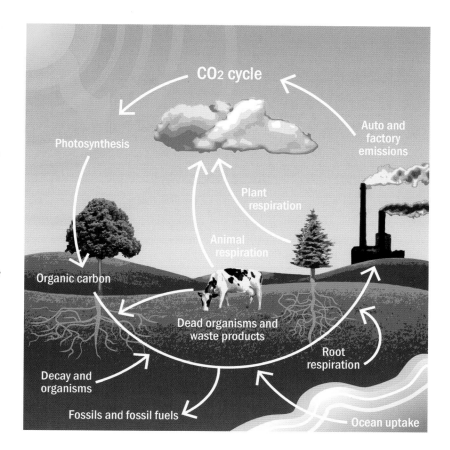

Carbon stores in trees and branches, and in soil. ▶

The soil – living, breathing and feeding plants

▲ When working on garden beds, we walk on boards to prevent compaction and preserve air pockets and soil structure.

When things go wrong in the garden the symptoms from above, the yellowing leaf, the stunted fruit or the insect infestation are what grabs our attention.

Yet the majority of our successes and failures in the garden have underlying causes that lie hidden in the soil. I encourage you to use your spade as a diagnostic tool. As gardeners, getting to know our soil is fundamental. Most plants when plucked from soil do not survive long. We are all aware that the mineral and organic elements of soil provide plants with essential nutrients, yet this is only a fraction of what plants need from soil.

Plants function with distinct tops and bottoms, soil gives roots anchorage. The soil provides the water and oxygen roots need to respire. Soil acts as insulation against temperature extremes. For our plants to prosper, we need to insure all these needs are met. Soils consist of mineral particles and organic matter, with the pores between filled with either water or air. The variety of soils reflects the distinct parent material, vegetation and climate in which they were formed.

Soil texture

We categorise soils according to their texture. Soil texture is based on the particle size of the mineral elements. Moisten some of your soil and rub it in the palm of your hand.

A sandy soil has larger particles and will feel gritty. If you attempt to roll it into a sausage it will crumble and have no plasticity. A clay soil has very fine particles, will feel sticky or slippery and will form a sausage when rolled.

Between the extremes of sand and clay lie loams that possess a balance of clay and sand particle and silts composed of fine, silky particles. Sandy or light soils are easily dug (lifting potatoes is a joy) and they are free draining. Conversely, they retain little water, are leached of nutrients and easily eroded by wind or rain.

Clays have the advantage of retaining water for long periods, likewise storing high amounts of nutrients that are available to plants. However, as any gardener with a bad back will tell you, they are hard to dig, prone to water logging in winter and rock hard in summer.

SOIL TYPE	ADVANTAGES	PROBLEMS	IMPROVEMENTS
SAND	• Free draining. • Resist compaction. • Easily dug.	• Poor water and nutrient holding. • Easily eroded. Low humus levels.	• Addition of organic matter. • Addition of clay or clay-like bentonite. • Mulching.
CLAY	• Often high in nutrients. • Able to store water and nutrients.	• Compact easily. • Poor drainage. • Hard to dig.	• Addition of organic matter. • Gypsum (if sodic). • Avoid digging when wet. • Avoid compaction through traffic. Use boards on vegetable beds.
SILT	• Often high in nutrients.	• Compact easily	• Addition of organic matter.
LOAM	• Shares the advantages of both sand and clay.	• Possible compaction.	• Add compost as mulch. • Avoid traffic compaction.

The soil profile

Digging deep into the soil we often see a distinct banding of different coloured and textured material — the soil profile.

The topsoil tends to be darker, it is where the majority of organic matter and life is found.

Most root activity occurs in the top 15cm of the soil. The subsoil is less fertile and usually paler. There are few roots here, mainly from larger or more drought tolerant plants.

The parent material is the mineral element of the soil – weathered rock below which lies the parent rock itself.

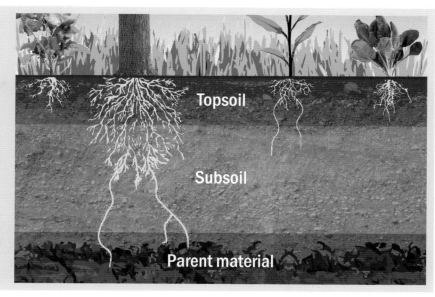

Topsoil

Subsoil

Parent material

The texture of our soil is difficult to alter without large inputs. It is possible to improve a sand by adding ¼ volume clay to the top soil but to improve a clay to loam would require adding more than 60% sand.

Soil structure

The aspect of the soil we can best tackle is the structure. Soil structure is the way the individual mineral and organic particles of the soil group together.

Humus is key to the formation of soil structure. Humus is that part of soil organic matter that has decomposed as far as possible and become stable; it is the ultimate carbon sink.

It is a dark sticky substance that gives good topsoil its rich colour and earthy smell. It acts as glue grouping soil particles into crumb. The colloidal chemistry of humus means it makes nutrients available to plant roots and improves water retention. As well as humus, mycorrhizal fungi are the living elements of the soil essential in forming pores between particles that allow the roots to receive water and oxygen; here the earth worm is the hero.

A good garden soil can be almost half pore space. From the plants perspective, a well structured soil has a crumb that is stable and doesn't breakdown in rain. It is loose enough to allow roots to grow and water, nutrients and oxygen to penetrate; if we squeeze a hand full of well structured soil it should noticeably reduce in volume. It has fine aggregates, good tilth rather than large clods.

A poorly structured soil collapses in rain and forms crusts, it is grouped in large clumps or sheets, it is hard to dig. It is inclined to water logging in winter and erodes easily.

Some of the poorest structured soils are the silts often bought in as top soil, they appear rich and fluffy when first applied but quickly compact to form a hardpan. Be very wary of buying in top soil. Unless carefully formulated it is often best, especially in environmental terms, to work with the existing soil and improve it or select plants adapted to it.

Hydroponics and soilless growing media

While good garden soil is perfect for growing plants in the ground, it is usually inadequate for growing plants in containers. When plants are grown in pots both their drainage and aeration are compromised by the confines of the container.

To achieve good aeration and drainage most growing media are soilless and based on sands or other inorganic elements of fairly coarse particle size combined with organic matter, pine bark or peat, to increase water and nutrient holding capacity.

The high organic content of potting mixes also helps to keep them light. The qualities of good drainage, aeration and high organic matter also have a downside. Growing medias drain so well they dry out easily and leach nutrients, and the high organic matter encourages fungi that produce waxy substances that repel water, making the mix hydrophobic.

To compensate, various water holding gels and wetting agents can be used. As home gardeners we need to be aware that our pot plants will dry out far more quickly than plants in the ground. The extreme end of soilless gardening is hydroponics, where all nutrients are provided in solution and the media becomes an inert free draining substance like Rockwool. From an organic perspective it is very hard to replicate the full suite of nutrients provided by a living soil.

I hope this encourages you to ask questions about your own soil and to ask those questions with a spade in your hand. Go out and have a dig around your garden, have a feel of your earth.

Nutrition – feed the soil, not the plants

▲ Heronswood's parterre has high organic levels from recycling compost, mulching and planting with blood and bone.

In nature there are no rich or poor soils. Wild plants are adapted to soils of their natural habitats. Their nutrient requirements are met by minerals from the parent rock and natural growth and decay.

Gardeners place extra demands on plants. We want them to grow outside of their natural range. To produce large crops we interfere with them by pruning, shaping and tidying away leaves. This is where fertilising comes in; to keep our plants at optimum growth we need to provide the optimum nutrition for our garden soil.

Nutrients are essential for a plant to carry out a normal life cycle. There are at least 16 essential elements. The most important of these – carbon, hydrogen and oxygen – are provided by air and water. The rest come from minerals in the soil and decaying matter. Nutrients are needed for different plant functions – any deficiency or excess results in a vast range of specific symptoms.

Most soils provide the majority of nutrients but, because plants are constantly drawing them from the soil, they must be replenished. The main nutrients that need continual replenishing are nitrogen (N), phosphorus (P) and potassium (K) – the 'N:P:K' listed on fertiliser labels.

A good compost will provide most of these requirements and the majority of soils deliver most other nutrients at adequate levels. However, Australia's ancient soils are notoriously low in phosphorus.

If soil is nutrient deficient it is best to address this when establishing a garden bed by adding compost and fertiliser and then maintaining this level

Fertilising is not a matter of just adding more nutrients. Plant growth is limited by the supply of the scarcest nutrient. Many gardeners make the mistake of just adding more and more fertiliser; you can have too much of a good thing.

For example, nitrogen rich urea makes a lawn green but when applied in excess, say by a leg-cocking canine, it can burn and kill. By using compost as the main fertiliser it is very hard to over-fertilise our gardens.

Nutrients also react one with each other. For instance, copper aids in processing nitrogen. Also, nutrients need to be present in forms that plants can access – this is determined by chemical form, soil moisture and pH.

Only fertilise when plants are actively growing

Applying fertiliser is about timing and knowing the needs of your plants. Plants only require fertilising when they are actively growing. For most this means fertilising in autumn and spring. In spring, use a fertiliser high in nitrogen to encourage leaf growth. In autumn, use phosphorous and potassium to strengthen the plant and encourage root development. Nutrients are delivered through moisture in the soil. In summer there is no point in fertilising dry ground – drought affected plants are more likely to be harmed than helped by fertiliser. Always fertilise moist soil and water after application.

We also need to synchronise our fertilising with the life cycle of our plants. Fertilise with a high nitrogen fertiliser to encourage initial growth and leafy foliage. To encourage fruit set and ripening, back off the nitrogen and use a fertiliser higher in potassium and phosphorus (look for the relative levels of N:P:K on the fertiliser packet).

Like people, plants have different eating requirements. Those adapted to sandy, low nutrient soils are light feeders often requiring no extra fertiliser. Many food plants are gross feeders, especially leafy vegetables and fruits like citrus.

These plants will need regular composting and fertilising. They may also need direct boost. In organics this is best delivered as a foliar feed delivered straight to the leaves to avoid leaching through the soil.

Our vegetable parterre is on a sandy loam. Every new display (3 times a year) we take the opportunity to fork in blood and bone and bentonite clay. We dress the soil with organic pig manure and our compost. When working on the beds we walk on boards, to prevent compaction and preserve air pockets and the structure of the soil. At Heronswood we are aiming to close the nutrient cycle by focusing on compost rather than purchased inputs.

We have sandy soils but with years of improvement, through compost and mulching, we have good levels of organic matter. We do not fertilise our kikuyu lawn, clippings are left, so no nutrients are being removed. All garden beds are fed through mulching with compost in spring. The more intensive production and flower beds receive additional applications of Diggers Organic Veggie & Herb fertiliser in spring and Diggers Organic Fruit & Citrus as flowers and fruit are forming and again in winter.

Rock dust is applied sparingly to ensure supply of micronutrients. Leaf vegetables and flowers in early growth are given organic foliar fertiliser and liquid seaweed every 2-3 weeks. However, we do not have a fixed schedule. We look to the plants and the weather to guide us. By not overfertilising we avoid pests attracted by sappy leaf growth and limit our impact on the surrounding waterways.

We feed the soil, not the plant

Following an organic approach to soil fertility, we let the soil itself sort out the complex requirements of the plants. We feed the soil, not the plant. Rather than treating specific symptoms with a specific product we take an holistic approach to soil health. Organic fertilising is like the Slow Food of fertilising versus the Fast Food of the synthetic fertiliser industry.

Synthetic fertilisers are quick fixes; they rely on their volatility to be readily accessible to plants. They move rapidly through the environment, washing into waterways, causing algal blooms and degradation of aquatic environments.

Organic fertilisers are slowly released into the soil. They are less concentrated and tend to come in a form bulked out by organic matter that also helps to improve the structure of the soil.

pH explained

pH is the measure of the Potential Hydrogen in the soil.

In lay terms, it indicates how sweet (alkaline) or sour (acidic) a soil is. The range is from 1-14 and one point equals a tenfold increase or decrease. pH 7 is neutral. Below 7 the soil is acidic, above 7 the soil is alkaline.

pH tests are simple to use and a good first step when creating a new garden bed. pH affects the availability of nutrients to plants. At high or low levels nutrients become "locked up" in the soil or, alternatively, available at toxic levels that affect plant growth. Most plants prefer a neutral pH. In organic gardening pH is moderated by the increase of organic matter in the soil. Lime can be added to raise pH in acid soils.

Alkaline soils are found in limestone areas and are hard to correct organically. Here, increase organic matter to encourage soil life and add iron chelate (organic certified form) to reduce yellowing of leaves caused by pH induced iron deficiency.

It's easy to select plants for your soil type rather than adding a lot of soil amendments.

Organic fertilisers are generally recycled products like manures, straws and composts, repurposing what would otherwise be waste. Synthetic fertilisers require large amounts of energy and fossil fuel to produce, negating many of the carbon benefits of the plants they fertilise. Keeping garden soil fertile is about providing it with a well-rounded meal, not junk food and vitamin pills.

Remember, the nutrients we feed our garden soil are ultimately the nutrients we are feeding ourselves!

ACID TOLERANT	ALKALINE TOLERANT
Azaleas/Rhododendrons	Beetroot
Berries	Brassicas
Potatoes	Iris
Camellias	Onions/Leeks
Rhubarb	Asparagus
Carrots	Lavender
Watermelon	Olives
	Lettuce
	Bay

A simple pH test

1. Place a sample of soil on a saucer and add a few drops of dye indicator.

2. Mix well and form a paste.

3. Dust with Barium Sulphate and wait a minute or two for the colour to emerge.

4. Use the colour chart to match colours and determine the pH of your soil sample.

Composting – making soils and mulches

▲ Nutrient rich, home made compost.

Composting is an essential component of organic gardening. It recycles our waste, improves soil structure, fertilises and inoculates our soil with beneficial organisms.

Composting is a natural process, yet successful composting often eludes the home gardener.

We have all experienced the smelly heap or the dry heap that keeps growing but never seems to produce a usable end result. At Heronswood (and St Erth) we have fairly constant success by using a simple aerobic method and following some basic rules, just like baking a cake or, more appropriately, brewing beer.

The site

In a suburban situation the position of a compost heap would be limited. It would ideally have some shading in summer. It should have easy access both in terms of depositing waste and removing compost.

We have two composting areas – one near our kitchen garden, the other in the ornamental garden – so we can make our compost near where it is to be used. Both our compost areas are in part shade and rest on soil or mulch.

Compost materials

The first phase of the composting process is gathering the compost material. For us and most gardeners the decision of what to compost is made for us by the garden waste we have at hand.

At Heronswood we use prunings, weeds, spent organic potting mix, vegetable kitchen scraps, coffee grounds, lawn clippings and chook poo from cleaning the hen house.

Materials we avoid composting are:

- Any plant material that has a serious persistent disease, especially if from the *Solanaceae* (tomatoes, potatoes).

- Bulbous weed material like oxalis that will not be easily killed by the composting process (we are experimenting with drowning the bulbs in a barrel before composting).

- Avoid too many weed seeds or perennial weeds like kikuyu or tradescantia if you are not confident of reaching temperatures of 55°C or more.

- Avoid meats and other obvious rodent food in an open heap.

It is vital to see the gathering and sorting of the waste material as a separate step to the actual making of the compost.

We have at least three bays working. One with the raw material, another in which the compost pile is made and a third into which the compost is turned and left to mature.

Confusing a working compost heap with a pile of random dumped garden waste is one of the primary causes of failure in compost making. For good, quick composting you need to ensure that material is added according to its carbon (C) and nitrogen (N) ratio.

The ideal C:N ratio lies between 20:1 and 40:1. As you can see compost requires far more carbon than nitrogen. Too much carbon will slow compost, while higher nitrogen heaps will lose nitrogen to the air in the form of smelly ammonias. You also need to balance the moisture content by adding wet material, like grass clippings, with dried wood prunings.

▼ Organic material with a Carbon:Nitrogen ratio greater than 20:1 will use up nitrogen in composting.

COMPOST MATERIAL	C:N RATIO
Cardboard	500:1
Straw	40-150:1
Leaves	30-80:1
Lawn clippings	18-21:1
Kitchen waste	15:1
Poultry manure with saw dust	9-11:1
Weeds	18-20:1

Making the compost heap – size matters!

A cubic metre seems to be the accepted minimum size for a heap. The mass of the heap and its surface to volume ratio limits heat loss. If a heap were to get much bigger than this oxygen supply to the centre would be compromised. We keep our heaps contained in bays that help maintain the heaps proportion and insulate the sides.

Just as the size of the heap matters so too does the size of the particles we put in the heap. At Heronswood our chipper transforms woody waste that has lain inert for weeks into a steaming pile. Any way you can mechanically reduce the size of the particles being composted will speed up the process. Once chipped the material is combined with grass clippings, soft weeds and vegetable cuttings in layers. Depending on the material we have at hand, if there is a lot of woody material, we sometimes add blood and bone as we go to increase the nitrogen level. By making sure we have a good ratio of compost materials we avoid pH problems, we don't add lime.

The breakdown process

Soon after being made the temperature in the heap rises as thermophillic, heat loving bacteria begin the breakdown process. Temperature in our heap reaches 55-60°C. It needs to remain this hot for a week to ensure all weed seeds and pathogens are killed.

To keep the temperature up we turn the heap several times. In turning the heap we try to invert the mix to ensure even heating, this is helped by turning the heap into a second bay. To ensure it is well aerated, we are careful not to compact the heap when we are forking it.

Keeping the heap moist is a challenge, especially in dry summers. We add water as needed when we turn the heap. Covering the heap is important to insulate it, thus maintaining moisture and temperature levels.

Making compost

1. A chipper makes light work of woody waste.

2. Once chipped, add it to the heap.

3. Grass clippings help balance moisture levels.

4. Turning the heap ensures even heating.

5. Good compost is dark and earthy.

6. Adding the finished compost to the Heronswood berry patch.

After two weeks the temperature drops and a new group of organisms, mainly fungi, now colonise the heap. It is in this phase that humus begins to develop. Once the heap reaches a stable ambient temperature it is left to mature and earthworms begin to colonise the heap.

The whole process takes several months. Timing varies depending if it's in the cool of winter or the heat of summer. Ideally, the final product is dark and smells earthy, with an even consistency and is weed and disease free. Occasionally, seeds like amaranth, or marigolds slip through. We apply the compost as mulch to our garden beds, letting the humic goodness percolate into the soil.

Pests and diseases

▲ Exclusion is a simple and effective form of pest management.

I worked in a retail nursery for years; I have the silhouette of customers carrying plastic bags of mouldy leaves burnt on my retina.

Inevitably the customer would present a nondescript pox-ridden leaf and demand a definitive diagnosis like "Delphinium Droop" and depart with an aerosol can proclaiming "for the treatment of Delphinium Droop" with which they could annihilate their foe. It's how many go to the doctor – they have bronchitis and want an antibiotic, not an analysis of their smoking habit.

There are military as well as medical overtones in how we talk about pests and diseases; terms like foe, battle, war and victory are hard to avoid. The military model is embedded in the agrochemical industry; remember Monsanto produced Agent Orange.

Sometimes in our desire to control our gardens we lose sight of why we are gardening. For most it's to produce healthy food, connect with nature and gain a sense of serenity. How can we do this if we see our gardens as battlegrounds? They should be as Michael Pollan extols; *"a place where we can meet nature halfway."*

Our gardens are part of a wider ecosystem and we are deluding ourselves that we can totally control our garden with weaponry or concoctions. A good gardener is more choreographer than commander.

Our actions seldom have specific results. Spraying "Delphinium Droop Destroyer" will affect more than the "droop." As annoying as pests can be it is more helpful to understand them than to demonise them.

Eradication of a pest or disease would inevitably come at economic as well as environmental cost; an arms race with no clear winners. Before we look at dealing with a perceived pest we need to look at acceptable levels.

This will vary from crop to crop and plant to plant. Salad vegetables are practically useless if too pock-marked or bronzed. However we may tolerate the same level of damage on an ornamental shrub at the back of a border.

Don't stress over every mark and blemish; learn to manage a pest population, not eradicate it.

The basis of good pest management is observation. When does the problem happen? Can I see and describe the suspected culprit? What plants are affected? In what season, time of day or type of weather? Is the soil wet or dry? Is the plant in shade or sun?

This kind of observational information is invaluable, especially when seeking expert advice. Also, the more you do this, the more you will become the expert, solving your own problems.

Most garden problems that are blamed on beetles, caterpillars and fungi have their root cause in poor plant health and plant selection. Before heading for the aerosol, check if plants are receiving adequate nutrition remembering that over supply, particularly of nitrogen, can be as hazardous as starvation.

Have you been rotating your vegetable crops? Is the plant in the right place? A rose in poorly ventilated shade will always be susceptible to black spot and aphids. This is a garden design problem not a pest problem.

One of the fundamental ways of preventing pests and diseases in the garden is hygiene. At the most basic, keep your tools clean. Soil-borne fungi like phytophthora devastate gardens and natural bush; they can travel on a dirty spade, even muddy boots.

Clean shovels with diluted bleach after digging out a dead or diseased plant. When you are pruning susceptible plants, disinfect your tools when moving between plants to minimise the potential spread of viruses, bacteria and fungi.

Remove and destroy diseased plants and avoid using them in compost unless you are totally confident in reaching consistently high temperatures in your heap.

In our Kitchen Garden we can't run the risk of building a population of the various tomato viruses, so, when we remove the bulk of spent plants post-harvest, they are not placed into the compost. Clean up rotting windfall. Keeping areas around high value or susceptible plants tidy can prevent pests getting a foothold.

We had a bit of a snail problem in our Herb Garden. After setting numerous, beery snail traps that dramatically reduced the problem, we only achieved final success when we cut back and tidied the surrounding rosemary and lavender – removing snails and their hidey-holes.

I must confess I really don't like squishing snails, but luckily at Heronswood we abdicate the responsibility of snailicide to our ducks. They devour them ecstatically. I prefer ecstatic ducks over chemicals any day. Exclusion is a particularly effective organic method of plant protection. Just as you protect your home with a lock rather than shooting potential thieves; instead of doing battle with what is dining on your plants, shut them out.

White garden netting is brilliant for keeping birds out of fruit trees and berries – being white and thick they can see it and are less likely to become entangled. Again the focus is to protect our crop, not really inflict damage on our competitors. Likewise, fine woven vegetable net strung over a frame allows us to grow brassicas when cabbage moths are active without having to spray.

Fruit cages are the ultimate exclusion method. They can be found in old country gardens where whole orchards and veggie plots are enclosed in mesh to protect them from the wildlife. In possum prone suburbs a fruit cage may be only way to get a crop. Copper sprays and tapes create effective non-toxic slug and snail barriers for precious seedlings.

In our parterre we uses a motion-activated, ultrasonic noise and light show called Animal Away to deter possums and birds from entering. It seems very effective; it can even deter keen eared small children!

▲ The ultimate snailicide!

Tidy up garden clippings to deter bugs that make piles of scraps their home. ▼

Clean pots, spades and garden tools will minimise the potential spread of disease. ▲

79

▲ LEFT When you need to spray Harlequin beetles target the bugs only, not the whole garden.

RIGHT Grow flowers like *Orlaya grandiflora* that beneficial insects need – Soldier beetles will feed on the eggs of pests like aphids.

The enemy of my enemy is my friend

Why go to the effort of killing pest insects when there are so many creatures that will do the work for you? All you need to do is provide them with suitable board and lodgings and luckily this can come in the form of ornamental flowers. Predator wasps, ladybirds, lacewings and other beneficial insects rely on pollen and nectar to provide the energy to reproduce and seek out prey.

Don't simply grow just any flowers, beneficial insects are particularly attracted to flowers from the *Apiaceae* (carrot/parsley) family, *Asteraceae* (daisy) family or the *Lamiaceae* (mint/sage) family. Flowers for beneficials include bronze fennel, Queen Anne's lace, borage, sweet alyssum and anise hyssop.

Think of sowing seasonal annual flowers with each vegetable sowing or sow Diggers Beneficial Insect Collection for year-round coverage. This is yet another reason to blur the line between your production and ornamental garden. Come-on you no-frills veggie growers, treat yourself to some flowers! You are not "going soft", you're killing pests in the nicest possible way.

Having encouraged you to look at your plant selection, maintenance regime and other holistic approaches there are times when you do need to take the direct approach. If particularly valuable or susceptible plants are under attack, the gloves are off!

When we have to go on the direct offensive against a pest it is best to be as targeted as possible, think drone strike rather than carpet bombing. Just because a treatment is organic does not mean we shouldn't apply it with the same care and precision as more noxious chemicals.

Pyrethrum is a brilliant non-selective organic insecticide; you can even grow your own. However, its effectiveness is why you should be very selective in its use.

If you have Harlequin beetles on your hollyhocks, just spray the Harlequin beetles, not the whole garden bed; you need to limit any friendly fire on your beneficial insects. Alternatively Diatomaceous Earth, actually fossilised algae, is very effective and specific in killing beetles through dehydration (it also controls slugs), yet remains inert in the soil.

Controlling harmful fungi in the garden is another example of when timely offensive action is needed. With humid weather, mildew and black spot can proliferate and when dealing with stone fruit, leaf curl is a perennial issue. Organic fungicides such Eco-fungicide and copper based Kocide give effective and timely control.

Traps are another way of targeting pests. Snail traps and codling moth lures are brilliant ways of controlling populations. We can even bring in hired mercenaries, beneficial organisms bought in for specific problems.

Often mistaken for a chemical, Dipel is actually a beneficial bacterium effective at killing moth and butterfly caterpillars that can ruin our leafy vegetables. There are numerous companies that sell beneficial bugs targeted for specific pests. These can be very useful especially for spider mites that are conventionally controlled with powerful chemicals.

There are great resources on the internet. Diggers website and encyclopedic texts like "What pest or disease is that" can be used to analyse specific problems and cures. What I would encourage gardeners to do is to think a bit more laterally and holistically before they reduce their garden problems to specific symptoms and cures.

As you become a good gardener, through good practice you never need be the pest and disease expert. As Michael Pollan observes it is when a gardener "respects and nurtures the wilderness of his soil and his plants that his garden seems to flourish most."

Ghost forest in the making ▲ — the red pine trees have succumbed to the mountain pine beetle.

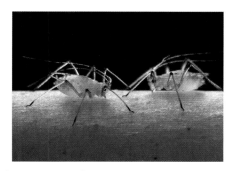

▲ FROM TOP TO BOTTOM Cane toad, cabbage moth, Queensland fruit fly and aphids.

Climate change, ghost forests and gardens

Changing climate will present gardeners with a new set of pest problems. The impact of rising temperature on insect populations and the environment is dramatically illustrated in the expanding ghost forests of North America (see photo above).

Great swathes of White pines have been decimated by booming populations of mountain pine beetles. The beetle is cold sensitive and susceptible species of pine like White and Jack pine have thrived at altitudes too cool for the beetle.

With consecutive warm seasons the beetles moved into higher altitudes, they have over wintered and turned vast areas of ancient pines into ghostly sentinels. Hundreds of years of embodied carbon are about to be released into the atmosphere.

Gardens are not immune to similar effects. The changes will be complex. There will be temporal changes to pests; warm season pests like aphids and cabbage moths will maintain populations over winter and attacks will start earlier.

Also, there will be spatial changes. The CSIRO predict that with warming in Australia, diseases and pests like the dreaded Queensland fruit fly will move southward.

The populations of existing species are also set to change. In southern Australia some species of cockchafers and mites seem to be expanding. Remember that beneficial insects will also be affected. In areas where summer rainfall is set to increase fungal diseases will boom, so more black spot on the roses!

It need not be all doom and gloom – some pest populations are shrinking. Army worms and pea weevil populations are decreasing in Southern Australia and some snail and slug populations are declining with drier conditions. As gardeners we will need to be more flexible in the timing of our planting and pest control measures and become more experimental in our approach.

Plant forms and life cycle

▲ Annuals live fast and die young.

Plants have vastly different life cycles that are reflected in a range of forms known as annuals, biennials and perennials.

Understanding these basic forms is more than an academic exercise, it's a powerful tool in getting the most from our plants. It comes down to knowing what a plant 'wants' to do and correlating this with what we want from a plant.

Annuals

Annuals live fast and die young. They last not so much for a year but a season. Their survival strategy is of avoidance. The key to their life cycle is the seed. Annuals cope with drought, cold and heat by living in the good times and focusing on the seed as the mechanism for the plant getting through the bad times. In seed form they can survive for millennia.

They are vulnerable plants and must reproduce as quickly and prolifically as possible. It is this "rock star" life cycle that makes them so valuable to us. They have no time to be coy, if they want their seeds pollinated and their fruit dispersed they have to get down to business and really flower and really fruit.

To get the most from annuals we need to keep the good times going for as long and consistently as possible. They are fair weather friends and at the hint of trouble, lack of water, a really cold or hot day they will bolt – go to seed.

So you need to know what they like and pander to that, especially if what you want are not seeds but leaves. Take coriander for example. It panics when it gets hot and runs to seed, its leaves become stunted and bitter. To keep it really leafy it's best grown in winter.

We can extend the useful life of annuals through dead heading, a delaying technique. However, if we are growing our annuals for seed or flower they need a bit of stress to trigger flowering. If we give them too much of a good thing, especially nitrogen rich fertilisers, they become all lush leaf and sappy, like Elvis with too many hamburgers.

The other thing about annuals is accepting that they won't live forever. Unless you are seed saving, don't let the sad fading display linger, get in and rip them out and start with the next planting. Nothing looks sadder than an aging rock star. When they go to the dark side annuals become the ultimate bad boys – weeds. To deal with annual weeds we need to trick the seeds into breaking their dormancy then ruthlessly dispatch the seedlings before they can set the next generation of seeds. This progressively reduces the seed bank in the soil.

Biennials

Biennials, as the name suggests, last for 2 growing seasons. They are the middle distance runner as opposed to the annual sprinter. The line between annual and biennial can be fuzzy, depending on climate variation and breeding. Breeders have tinkered with some foxglove cultivars, for example, to get them to flower within a season. Biennials, like annuals, are reliant on seeds for propagation but they usually have another means of coping with stress. Usually, this is in the form of a big root – think carrots and parsnips. Biennials use their first season of growth to produce leaves and store energy that helps get them through the winter and provide for seed production the following spring/summer.

Parsley lets us know when its time is up. You can get two years out of happy parsley but the first season's growth will be leafy and in the second season it's concentrating on stalks for seed heads. Some biennials we ruthlessly treat as annuals, silverbeet is an example, we want it for its youthful leaves not seeds. Likewise, onions we grow for the first season bulbs not the second year's flower.

Of course, if we are seed saving from biennials we need to be patient. If we are growing a biennial for its flowers however, we need to sow it a season before we want it to flower.

Biennial hollyhocks and foxgloves need to be planted as seeds the preceding spring or as seedlings before winter so they can go through their first season of vegetative growth to give them the power to flower. Even more than annuals we can be tempted into trying to get our biennials to last for ever, be bold and remove them and get on with the next season's planting.

Perennials

Perennials are plants with life cycles of more than two years. They sit out adversity rather than avoid it, they have various coping techniques. They might have waxy, furry or grey foliage to resist summer heat and drought. They might be deciduous to avoid the darkness and cold of winter.

They are not solely reliant on the seed to propagate, they have bulbs, stolons, roots and shoots that become new plants. A bit like biennials when grown from seed, perennials will not really start maturing until at least the next growing season. Perennials are divided into herbaceous and woody perennials.

Herbaceous perennials are the plants we associate with a perennial border. They all have soft annual stems and perennial roots and take various forms: ground covers, small shrubs, tufted lilies, ferns and grasses. They can be large – bananas are herbaceous perennials. Many popular herbaceous plants have evolved in prairies, steppes and Mediterranean regions where they are subject to grazing, drought, harsh winters and fire. Not only do they survive in these conditions – they thrive. One common method of dealing with grazing or cold is producing new shoots at their base.

Herbaceous perennials sacrifice their extremities. It is this survival technique that makes the constantly cut lawn a success. This ability to respond to cutting is a valuable tool for manipulating flowering with herbaceous perennials. By removing flowers or cutting plants to the ground we can extend or delay their flowering times.

Don't let the delicate flowers of delphinium Blue Sensation fool you – treat it mean after flowering and you will be rewarded with several repeat performances. Likewise many salvias, such as *Salvia nemorosa*, have a distinct clumping form and respond to well-timed hard pruning.

1. A typical herbaceous perennial, sedum flowers in summer.

2. Sedums die off dramatically in winter, leaving sculptural annual seed stems that are cut back to the ground.

3. New growth reveals that the sedum is alive and well, ready to grow new stems again in spring.

Many herbaceous perennials go through a semi-dormancy in winter. This is why many of Diggers perennials will arrive in winter with an "I am dormant" tag. The plant is very much alive, it's simply sitting winter out below ground. Sedums like Matrona and Autumn Joy dramatically demonstrate the winter die back. Many find the seed heads of sedums in winter to be sculptural and in areas with frost the old dead growth can provide protection to the base from the cold. So don't rush in to cut perennials too soon. The clumping form of many perennials can make propagating easy. By breaking up clumps we produce more plants, and reinvigorate the clump in the process.

Woody perennials

Woody perennials are the true marathon runners of the plant – world they form the dominant structural plants of our gardens, the trees and shrubs. Their wood or lignin allows these plants to grow large. They can compete with those fast living annuals by shading them and developing competitive root systems. When pruning woody perennials we need to be aware that this can have implications for many years to come. Likewise, because of their size in the landscape anything we do to them has implications for the plants that grow in their shade. The woody perennials are great carbon sinks, while we may be ruthless with annuals and herbaceous perennials we need to think long and hard before removing a mature tree or shrub.

Knowing the life cycle of the plants in our garden helps us to get the most from them. It also gives us confidence: no, you haven't killed that basil, it is naturally a one season wonder; be patient with your hollyhocks, they just need another season to flower, cut those salvias to the ground, they will come again.

Temperature – choosing the right plants

▲ Temperature initiates apple blossoms.

Temperature has a profound effect on plant growth. It is one of the most important schedulers of plant activity, of flowering, fruiting, budburst, initiation of roots in a cutting and the falling of autumn leaves.

Although other limiting factors like rainfall, light intensity and soil types play their part, climatic temperature variation from the poles to the equator is the great arbiter of what plants grow where.

Killer frosts and searing heat set the limits of where plants will survive. That we grow cherries in Tasmania and mangoes in Queensland is largely due to temperature.

As gardeners, understanding our local temperature range and seasonal fluctuations is the key to unlocking what we plant and when we plant it.

Hardiness and heat zones for perennials

The optimum temperature range for photosynthesis and respiration varies from plant to plant. Some have cell structures that tolerate freezing frosts, others can photosynthesise very efficiently above 30°C.

In nature, evolution has sorted out what plants grow where through thousands of years of adaptation to temperature and other environmental factors

We gardeners have a vast array of plant material, of seeds from every climate and region. It all looks appealing, juicy mangos and Blue Himalayan poppies. We do not have thousands of years of trial and error to work out what to plant in our patch.

In the US, the Department of Agriculture (USDA) conceived a series of plant hardiness zones based on the range of average annual minimum temperature. This is the basis of the Cold Zones for Australia that The Diggers Club devised with the Bureau of Meteorology.

However, the problem with looking at Cold Zones alone can be seen by glancing at the Diggers Cold Zones map. Here you will find that Hobart and Alice Springs share the same Cold Zone (9b). Clearly plants in both areas will need to be frost hardy. Yet the difference in summer heat is profound.

The major cause of plant failure in Australia is heat

Unlike gardens in England, northern Europe and the USA, gardens in Sydney, Adelaide and Perth have at least 30 days over 30°C compared with none (on average) in the UK.

So selecting plants for heat tolerance is crucial to gardening success. Unfortunately, nursery labels and selection guides give hopelessly inadequate information to make plant choice successful.

For example, Yates Garden Guide simplistically groups climates into tropical, sub-tropical and temperate. Tomatoes come from lowland tropics in South America.

They can be grown in temperate areas but not during 15°C temperatures. They won't set fruit in the tropics when temperatures are above 30°C. So their growing range is described by number of weeks over 15°C and below 30°C – which means all climates, but within this temperature range.

Only a fool or eternal optimist would base their Alice Springs garden on the plants that they saw thriving at the Botanical Gardens in Hobart.

This is why organisations such as Diggers and the American Horticultural Society have paired Cold Zones with Heat Zones. These 14 heat zones are divided according to the number of days above 30°C.

If we take heat into account we now see that Hobart is in Heat Zone 1 and Alice Springs in Zone 12. Selecting your plants then involves checking that they fit with both your Heat and Cold Zone

Microclimates

Remember that the temperature zones are simplifications. Some plants may be particularly affected by cold if it occurs early in winter before they have hardened off but tolerate later frosts or one day of frost but not repeated occurrences – all this detail is lost in the abstraction.

If we come down from the broad scheme of temperature zones to our backyard, we get to the level of micro-climates.

We all know we have a sunny spot for sitting in winter and a cool nook for escaping summer heat. The western side of our house bakes in the afternoon sun, the south is shaded and cool, to the east warmth in the morning is tempered by afternoon shade, and to the north heat is maximised.

As home gardeners we can experiment with crops outside their regular zone as our livelihood is not riding on their success.

Use microclimates to push the range of plants you can grow, experiment as they have done at the Royal Tasmanian Botanic Gardens growing bananas against a warm wall.

I have a long suffering coffee plant that was nearly killed by frosts when I moved to Melbourne's western plains.

Simply by moving it a few metres and under a north facing verandah it rewarded me with a handful of coffee beans! The other obvious way of extending the range of plants is with shelters, tunnels, cloches and shade houses.

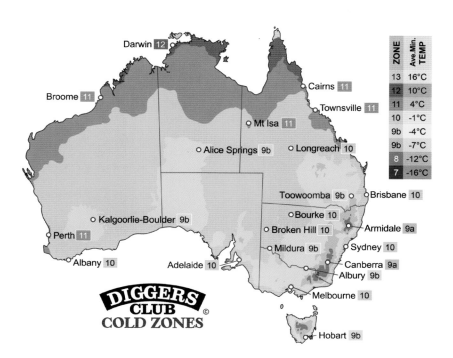

ZONE	Ave.Min. TEMP
13	16°C
12	10°C
11	4°C
10	-1°C
9b	-4°C
9b	-7°C
8	-12°C
7	-16°C

DIGGERS CLUB © COLD ZONES

Plant hardiness

The term 'hardy' is the root of much confusion. Some of this stems from the fact that, while it is a general term that can mean drought hardy or heat hardy to some and cold hardy to others, for many horticulturists it has a very specific meaning. Possibly reflecting its origins in the cooler climes of Britain and North America, plant hardiness refers to cold hardiness.

You may think cold hardiness is irrelevant in our sunburnt country, surely drought and heat hardy are more important? Yet even in Australia frosts and winter cold set the ultimate limit of what we can grow. For those who experience frost you will know the instant death frost brings to tender plants.

Much garden advice is based on the use of climate zones, (tropical, sub-tropical and temperate). This is not so useful for selecting individual plants, as there are many plants whose tolerances extend beyond their original climate zone. Also by timing our plantings we can avoid the extremes by planting tropical plants as annuals in temperate zones using growing days as a guide.

Simply using plant hardiness as a guide gives gardeners a wider and more accurate repertoire of plants to use in their garden.

Hardy Perennial/Annual/Biennial is a plant that can survive frost. This includes perennials whose exposed parts may die back over winter.

Tender Perennial/Annual/Biennial is a plant that cannot survive frost without protection.

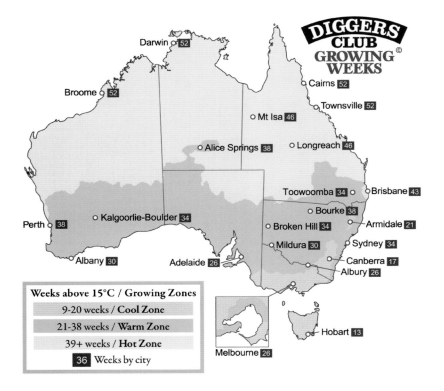

Weeks above 15°C / Growing Zones

9-20 weeks / **Cool Zone**	
21-38 weeks / **Warm Zone**	
39+ weeks / **Hot Zone**	
36 Weeks by city	

COOL SEASON crops from temperate, frosty areas [10-15°C soil temperatures] include ROOTS, LEAVES and SEEDS.

WARM SEASON crops from sub-tropical or tropical areas [15-25°C soil temperatures] include FRUITS.

Annual vegetables need accurate sowing temperatures

However, most of our vegetable crops are annuals and adapt to extremes of hot and cold by avoidance, adapting to particular seasons. Not being perennial plants we choose to sow them at the preferred temperature for germination – e.g. 10-15°C for cool weather crops and 15°C+ for warm weather crops (like tomatoes, zucchini and melons).

Seasonal fluctuations in temperature are the major determinate in sowing dates. The Diggers Club *Sow What When* chart gives detailed information on when to sow seeds for your particular climate. The broadest division of plants based on temperature is cool and warm season crops. Understanding this is fundamental to successfully time your planting.

Cool season crops are typically grown for their roots (carrots, parsnip and turnips), leaves (lettuce, cabbage, kale and spinach) or immature flowers (artichokes, broccoli and cauliflower). Only a few cool season crops are grown for their seeds (peas and broad beans).

These plants can endure short periods of frost once established. The low temperatures reduce energy use and increase sugar storage making them sweet. At the sign of warmth they tend to turn bitter or bolt to seed at the expense of leaf and root.

Some, like cabbages, can be grown in warmer months but you will need to be constantly vigilant against water stress, insect attack and extreme heat.

Warm season crops are mainly grown for fruits (tomatoes, eggplants, capsicums, melons) and seeds (green beans, corn). They are tender plants – unless they are protected, don't plant them outside until the threat of frost is over.

Warm temperatures mean these crops are photosynthesising and respiring at their peak so they need regular irrigation and fertilising to avoid stress and produce a good crop. It is especially critical with warm season crops to consider the number of growing weeks – that is those weeks above 15°C.

Check your sowing zone on the Diggers Growing Weeks map – Cool (9-20 weeks), Warm (21-38) and Hot (39+ weeks). While temperatures may be adequate to sow seeds you need to be sure that you have enough growing weeks to bring them to maturity.

This is critical when planting in cool zones. If you are planting tomatoes in Hobart be sure you select a variety and planting date that suits your available growing season. Think about extending the season by starting your plants indoors.

The big chill – number of chilling hours to fruit

Deciduous fruits add another layer of complexity. Many have evolved in climates with severe winters. If they were to flush with growth simply at the first sign of warmth, they could be fooled out of dormancy by an unseasonably warm winter's day only to lose all their fruit when the cold returns. To avoid this, these fruits really need to know they have gone through the worst of winter before they break dormancy.

To do this they need varying hours and intensity of winter chill (typically between 5 -10°C).

This is critical when selecting our fruit varieties in Australia where most of us experience warmer winters. If the buds do not receive sufficient chilling temperatures during the winter to completely release dormancy, the result is reduced fruit set and reduced fruit quality.

Diggers provides a range of "low chill" varieties such as White Satin nectarine. If you don't get adequate winter chill you might even consider our Low Chill Orchard collection. Chill factors can also influence the breaking of dormancy in seeds adapted to cold winters.

Do some research and see if chilling may improve the germination rate of seeds you are sowing.

Climate change and your garden

The fact that planning our gardens is so reliant on predicting our climatic condition means that climate change will inevitably affect what we grow and when we grow it.

For many, water restrictions have highlighted the changing rainfall patterns. Yet changes to our temperature mean we have more than drought to worry about. Entire climate zones are on the move. The Arbor Day Foundation has created a dramatic animation of the shifting in hardiness climate zones in the USA from 1990 to 2006 (see more information and maps below).

Similar changes are no doubt happening in Australia. The Bureau of Meteorology is predicting that 2013 is on track to be the warmest year on record. Anecdotal evidence suggests plant confusion. A Facebook post from a friend in Adelaide shows a picture of fruit forming on her peach in August.

Lesley from Kaydale Bulbs in Tassie commented in an email:

"As to climate change, for us here in the mountains of Tasmania, gardening has always been a challenge and the catch phrase global warming had an appealing ring to it. We always thought that our area could do with a couple of extra degrees (Mum had always hoped to be able to have a fig tree and lemons).

We have found the reality to be not just so cut and dried, we are not getting the depth of snow but the mood swings of the weather are more pronounced. This year things have been a lot earlier, making mulching fun (hence tiptoeing through like a pixie!) with some of the spring bulbs a good week or two earlier."

I think Lesley's point about the unpredictability of our seasons is important. As gardeners it is vital that we share our experiences so we can make sense of fundamental temperature shifts that may affect the very what, when and how of gardening.

Climate change has already altered hardiness zones

When the Arbor Day Foundation reviewed its hardiness zones for the US in 2006 they found conditions were considerably warmer than they had been in 1990.

When they checked their climate data it showed that areas covering many states had changed by one whole hardiness zone (Australian zones are largely confined to zones 9 & 10).

The changes are dramatically illustrated on an animated map found at their website – look for Hardiness Zones under the Media tab at:

www.arborday.org

The implications for tree planters is the trees that should be planted now are not the trees traditionally suited to an area but ones adapted to at least one hardiness zone warmer.

Thus predictive planting for changing climate will increasingly become part of the process for plant selection for all gardeners.

Hardiness zone images courtesy of the Arbor Day Foundation.

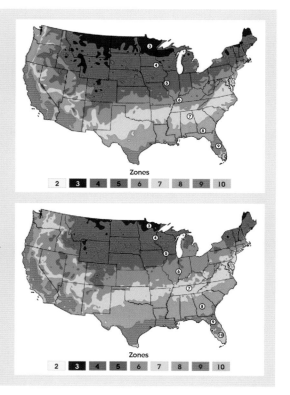

INSPIRING GARDENS

THE GARDEN OF ST ERTH

▲ Summer border, mostly herbaceous perennials.

Dry climate garden, mostly hardy evergreen pernnials. ▼

Plant selection and plant suitability

At our Heronswood garden we have been trialling and discarding plants as unsuitable since 1978. We don't want plant failures in our gardens and certainly not in yours.

Plants fail due to excessive heat, excessive cold, too much or too little water, excessive or too little light.

Our Diggers climate guides for plant selection are the most advanced in the world, being Australian climate adaptations of USDA Cold Zones and Heat Zones. Just pick up any nursery plant label or any guide on climate in our national magazines and see for yourself. Australia's inadequate climate information for plants hasn't improved in 60 years.

Most of the growing advice that comes from the highly respected RHS in the UK is deficient too because they ignore heat and water stress. Let me explain. "UK broadcast warning. *Heat wave coming – temperatures are expected to exceed 30°C!"*

Well, Darwin and the top 20% of Australia have every day over 30°C, all 365 days, so it is a fact that about 95% of Australia is hotter than the UK. Perth and Brisbane have 45 days whilst Melbourne, Sydney and Adelaide have 30-45 days over 30°C.

My guess is about 90% of plants that survive in the UK have little chance of survival here, except of course in gardens near the alps or in Tasmania and New Zealand's South Island.

Heat waves compound and lead towards water stress in our soils and excessive radiation on plant tissue. Over 70% of Australia is defined as a desert. So please read our climate guides carefully, identify the Heat and Cold Zone where you live and be sure to only select plants that we recommend for growing in that zone.

We believe, after 33 years of trials, this PLANT SELECTOR is the most complete guide for our harsher climate.

Heirloom annuals and perennials

Modern plant breeders have so dwarfed our traditional cottage annuals and perennials for suburban gardeners that we have discarded them. Our selections predate modern plant breeding, hence they are called heirloom flowers.

The best plants for Australian gardens

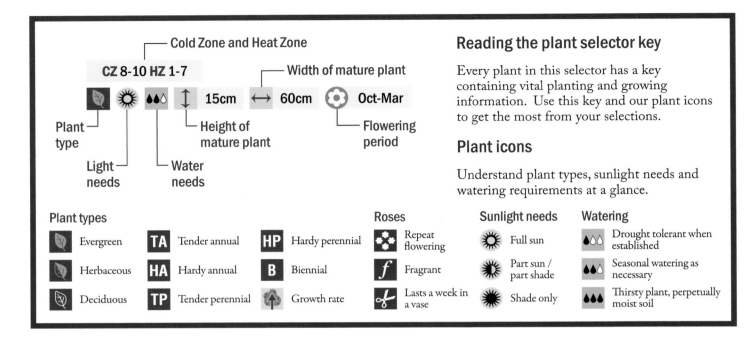

Reading the plant selector key

Every plant in this selector has a key containing vital planting and growing information. Use this key and our plant icons to get the most from your selections.

Plant icons

Understand plant types, sunlight needs and watering requirements at a glance.

Cold Zone and Heat Zone
CZ 8-10 HZ 1-7

Width of mature plant
15cm ↔ 60cm | Oct-Mar

Plant type

Light needs

Water needs

Height of mature plant

Flowering period

Plant types

Evergreen	TA Tender annual	HP Hardy perennial	
Herbaceous	HA Hardy annual	B Biennial	
Deciduous	TP Tender perennial	Growth rate	

Roses
- Repeat flowering
- Fragrant
- Lasts a week in a vase

Sunlight needs
- Full sun
- Part sun / part shade
- Shade only

Watering
- Drought tolerant when established
- Seasonal watering as necessary
- Thirsty plant, perpetually moist soil

To provide permanence in an ornamental garden we need to treat short lived annuals and short flowering period bulbs as ephemerals in the sense that they provide decorative highlights and not the substance that makes a garden interesting every month of the year.

All plants listed in our selector have been grown in our gardens at Heronswood or St Erth and photos and descriptions are based on our personal experience of gardening in different climate zones for over 33 years.

Most of our plants are available in our mail order magazines and at www.diggers.com.au

▼ Diggers magazines provide seasonal gardening advice and seed and plant selections from this Plant Selector.

A 'perennial' plant is one that lives from year to year as a permanent plant. An 'annual' is a plant that lives for one season only, growing from seed, flowering, setting new seed and dying in less than one year.

We need to choose plants that are perennials, particularly those that integrate well with others and have interesting foliage or a decorative form with subtle flowers, unlike impulse bedding plants that are annuals with overly large flowers that overload and tire the senses.

Our **Plant Selector** breaks these "first choice garden plants" into:

- **GROUND COVERS** — under 40cm tall.
- **EVERGREENS** — perennial plants with year-round foliage.
- **PERENNIALS** — permanent roots with foliage that dies down in the cool season.
- **SHRUBS** — compact, woody perennials, deciduous and evergreen.
- **CLIMBERS** — large, woody perennials, deciduous and evergreen.
- **EPHEMERAL BULBS** — seasonal flower interest with lengthy dormancy periods.
- **DIRECT SOW ANNUALS** — single season show, sow fresh seed each year.

A note on ground covers

It is essential that gardeners use plants not only to cover bare ground but to smother annual weeds before they get established. Ground cover plantings build up microflora to increase soil carbon by photosynthesis which also increases the water holding capacity. Many selections came from alpine regions which have rocky rubble for soil which raises soil temperatures so they are adapted to thriving in hot and cold conditions.

Drought tolerance

To reduce water use and increase survivability about 70% of our selections are drought tolerant (indicated by the ⬤ 1 drip icon). By reducing water use on ornamentals we can water our fruit and vegetables that need a continuous supply (indicated by the ⬤ 3 drip icon).

Cold Zones 7-13

Every plant in this selector is coded for its climate suitability i.e. survivability to extreme cold, frost hardiness (see page 85 for a larger Australian Cold Zones map).

ZONE	Ave.Min. TEMP
13	16°C
12	10°C
11	4°C
10	-1°C
9b	-4°C
9b	-7°C
8	-12°C
7	-16°C

Heat Zones 1-14

To survive extreme heat, be sure to identify your garden's climate zone as this selection is vital to gardening success. Heat Zones are based on the average number of days over 30°C per year.

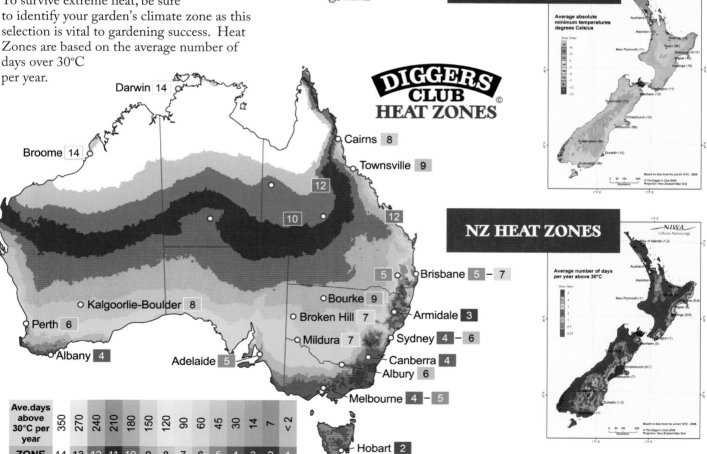

Ave.days above 30°C per year	350	270	240	210	180	150	120	90	60	45	30	14	7	<2
ZONE	14	13	12	11	10	9	8	7	6	5	4	3	2	1

91

Ground covers under 40cm

In our hot, dry climate it is a gardeners first task to cover the soil to retain moisture and to prevent weeds from getting started. All plants recycle carbon and it is vital to cover the soil with perennial soil smotherers quickly.

Sun Rose

Candytuft

Artemisia Valerie Finnis

Oregano KENT BEAUTY

Campanula poscharskyana

Chinese Plumbago

Ceratostigma plumbaginoides — Not the sprawling tall blue summer shrub we are familiar with, but a ground carpeting perennial with similar brilliant blue flowers and leaves that turn red with autumn colour changes.

CZ 7-10 HZ 1-10

🍃 ☀ 💧 ↕ 40cm ↔ 30cm ⊙ Oct-Mar

Oregano Kent Beauty

Origanum rotundifolium x scabrum — Exuding the pungent scent of oregano, this tidy plant is smothered in hop-like flower bracts that conceal tiny pink flowers. Tough and drought tolerant, the perfect ornamental for pots, hanging gardens and as a ground cover.

CZ 7-10 HZ 1-10

🍃 ☀ 💧 ↕ 20cm ↔ 50cm ⊙ Feb-Apr

Sun Rose

Aptenia cordifolia — The fastest, rich-green leaved ground cover we know for smothering weeds under pine trees, hanging down rockeries or providing edible garnishes. A perennial fleshy succulent from South Africa with 1.5cm bright-pink flowers. It survived Heronswood's restaurant fire – how tough is that?!

CZ 7-10 HZ 1-7

🍃 ☀☀ 💧 ↕ 5cm ↔ 1m ⊙ Dec-Feb

Artemisia Valerie Finnis

A. ludoviciana — Thriving on the dry side of the Rocky Mountains, it is well adapted to drought and cold with broad silvery leaves and columns of white flowers. We keep it clipped as a silver carpet to offset mounding green perennials in pastel colour schemes.

CZ 8-11 HZ 1-12

🍃 ☀ 💧 ↕ 40cm ↔ 60cm ⊙ Dec-Jan

Campanula poscharskyana

A vigorous, soil smothering campanula with exquisite star-shaped bluebell flowers. Perfect for colonising rockeries, steps or even shady nooks. The blue or white flowers carpet the ground for months.

CZ 8-10 HZ 1-7

🍃 ☀☀ 💧 ↕ 15cm ↔ 60cm ⊙ Oct-Mar

Candytuft

Iberis sempervirens — Candytuft flowers begin at the first hint of spring with perfect low profile blooms. Cool, lacy heads of the purest white suit rockeries or grow as a ground cover amongst spring bulbs.

CZ 8-10 HZ 1-8

🍃 ☀☀ 💧 ↕ 15cm ↔ 60cm ⊙ Aug-Oct

Catmint Snowflake

Nepeta x faassenii — This dwarf form of catmint with white flowers combines aromatic grey foliage in a short form for carpeting rose beds or edging a flower border. A tough plant that's drought and heat tolerant.

CZ 7-10 HZ 1-10

🍃 ☀ 💧 ↕ 30cm ↔ 30cm ⊙ Oct-Mar

Erodium

Part of the Geranium family from the calcareous soils of Spain and Greece that have a long flowering period. The striking flowers resemble larger flowered geraniums.

- Cotsworld Cream *E. chrysanthum* — Pale yellow flowers on dissected silver-green leaves.

- Spanish Eyes *E. glandulosum* — Veined lilac pink flowers with dark purple eyes.

CZ 8-10 HZ 1-9

🍃 ☀ 💧 ↕ 20cm ↔ 30cm ⊙ Sep-Apr

Erodium COTSWOLD CREAM

Chinese Plumbago

Erodium SPANISH EYES

Catmint SNOWFLAKE

Convolvulus sabatius

Seaside Daisy

Pink Evening Primrose combined with blue Catmint WALKERS LOW

Dianthus COTTAGE PINKS

Dianthus caryophllus x D. plumarius — Spiky, silver heat loving foliage for edging, with exquisitely perfumed, clove scented flowers on short stems (unlike florist carnations that fall over) that look good both in the garden and picked for the vase.

- BECKY ROBINSON — Old fashioned, pink with red markings on the margins.
- DORIS — Classic, long flowering, clove scented pale-pink with darker centres.
- MRS SINKINS — Best known, old fashioned in pink or white.

CZ 7-10 HZ 1-9

  ↕ 20cm ↔ 30cm ⊙ Oct-Dec

Evening Primrose

Oenothera speciosa — An exuberant, cheery and generous display. Evening primrose flowers last all day, with a progression of flowers continuing all summer if cut back. Combines exquisitely with catmint Walkers Low. Plant in a pot on the porch or as an edging along the drive. Smaller, darker pink available too.

CZ 8-11 HZ 1-10

☀ ⬧⬧⬧ ↕ 30cm ↔ 50cm ⊙ Nov-Apr

Geranium

Most of the English favourites won't take the hot Australian sun but there are tough, reliable forms of geranium that survive 40°C days hailing from New Zealand and South Africa.

- *G. incanum* — Delicate filigree foliage.
  ↕ 40cm ↔ 60cm
- SEA SPRAY *G. traversii* — Carpet of bronze leaves with pale pink flowers from NZ's Chatham Island. ↕ 15cm ↔ 30cm

CZ 8-10 HZ 2-7   ☀ ⊙ Sep-May

Convolvulus sabatius

A vigorous, weed smothering groundcover that hangs down walls. Perfect for pots too.

CZ 9a-11 HZ 1-10

☀ ⬧⬧⬧ ↕ 10cm ↔ 1m ⊙ Sep-Apr

Seaside Daisy

Erigeron karvinskianus — The miniature daisy that never stops flowering. Dusty pink flowers fade to white. Grows well in concrete cracks, rockeries and coastal sandy soil.

CZ 7-10 HZ 1-9

☀ ⬧⬧⬧ ↕ 15cm ↔ 30cm ⊙ Sep-May

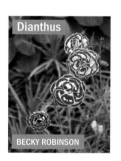
Dianthus BECKY ROBINSON

Dianthus MRS SINKINS

Dianthus DORIS

Geranium SEA SPRAY

Geranium incanum

How many plants do I need?

↕ Height   ↔ Spread

When buying and planting you should space plants at our recommended distances. Each plant description includes mature height and spread — evening primrose, for instance, has a height of 30cm and a spread of 50cm. To work out how many plants will cover one square metre, divide the <u>area</u> by the <u>spread</u> (i.e. $1.0m^2$ / $0.5m \times 0.5m$) and you will find you need 4 plants, or 16 plants for $4m^2$.

You can save a great deal of money by selecting perennials that **cover large areas** — choose *Euphorbia wulfenii, Gypsophila, Helichrysum petiolare,* Russian sage or wormwood — and that **multiply readily** — choose *Achillea, Anemone japonica,* evening primrose, lamb's ears and salvia rather than bulbs (they cover much larger areas and flower considerably longer). It takes 100 daffodils to cover the same area as one *Gypsophila*!

93

Sedum BERTRAM ANDERSON

Golden Marjoram

Stachys BIG EARS

Sedum VERA JAMESON

Snow in Summer

Verbena Polaris

Kalanchoe pumila

Sage PURPLE

Sage VARIEGATED YELLOW 'ICTERINA'

Golden Marjoram

Origanum vulgare 'Aureum' — Looks like a sunny day even when it is cloudy. A good carpeting gold leaved marjoram that loves heat, plus it can flavour a pizza too!

CZ 7-10 HZ 1-8

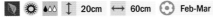 ☀ ☁ ↕ 20cm ↔ 60cm ⊙ Feb-Mar

Kalanchoe pumila

If every Australian garden had 20-30 perennials as good as this one, then our standards would lift dramatically. It is tough, extremely elegant (both in and out of flower), even after four days of 43°C without water. Spoon-shaped, toothed grey leaves fade to purple-grey and urn-shaped pink flowers look good in contrast to the foliage. Hardly ever needs watering as a potted plant.

CZ 9b-11 HZ 1-10

 ☀ ☁ ↕ 20cm ↔ 35cm ⊙ Jul-Nov

Sage

Salvia officinalis — Salvias offer outstanding variation in foliage colour, from common sage in the herb garden to purple or variegated foliage. They have both flavour and toughness, an excellent choice to enliven a herb garden.

- PURPLE SAGE — Matt purple leaves and blue flower spikes.
- VARIEGATED YELLOW — Yellow margins on sage-green leaves and lilac blue flowers.

CZ 7-11 HZ 1-8

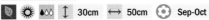 ☀ ☁ ↕ 30cm ↔ 50cm ⊙ Sep-Oct

Stachys Big Ears

Stachys byzantina — This large, macho felty leaf is about 5 times as big as the common lamb's ear and less tactile. It rarely flowers at Heronswood but it is indispensable as an edging plant in our evergreen border.

CZ 7-10 HZ 1-9

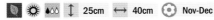 ☀ ☁ ↕ 25cm ↔ 40cm ⊙ Nov-Dec

Verbena Polaris

Verbena rigida — Pale lilac upright blooms love the sun and smother the weeds.

CZ 8-10 HZ 1-10

 ☀ ☁ ↕ 30cm ↔ 30cm ⊙ Nov-Mar

Sedum

Sedums hardly notice a week of 40°C days without water, flowering reliably. There are two sedums that make outstanding foliage or ground cover plants to contrast with the grey foliage of *Artemisia* 'Valerie Finnis' or *Achillea*.

- BERTRAM ANDERSON — A stunning deep purple foliaged ground cover with star-shaped pink flowers. ↕ 10cm ↔ 30cm
- VERA JAMESON — Greenish blue leaves and purple stems produce heads of pink flowers. ↕ 30cm ↔ 30cm

CZ 7-10 HZ 1-9  ☀ ☁ ⊙ Feb-Apr

Snow in Summer

Cerastium tomentosum — Wall to wall carpets of densely matted grey foliage with white flowers. Although vigorous, a clip with shears keeps it in shape. It's tough enough to sit on, cascade down a wall or a grow in rockery. Contrasts with vertical bearded iris or evergreen perennials.

CZ 7-10 HZ 1-9

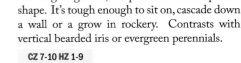 ☀ ☁ ↕ 15cm ↔ 1m ⊙ Oct-Dec

A well grown perennial can produce up to 10 times the number of flowers of one poorly grown. We always mulch with 4 inches of decomposed poultry manure in early spring because it smothers weeds and creates very rapid growth.

Australian natives

Many natives make outstanding ground covers, being perfectly adapted to excessive heat and dry conditions. Our selection adapts well with charming flowers that look natural and comfortable with non-natives from the Mediterranean like rosemary and lavender. Many are climbers or trailers, making them really economic to cover large areas.

Swan River Daisy

Sturt's Desert Pea

Running Postman

Kennedia prostrata — Brilliant red, pea-like flowers are eye catching in winter and early spring. Fast growing and ground hugging.

CZ 9a -10 HZ 1-10

🍃 ☼ ♦◊◊ ↕ 30cm ↔ 2m ⊙ Aug-Sep

Sturt's Desert Pea

Clianthus formosus — One of the most eye catching flowers in the world but a difficult plant to have success with. Germination is rapid and is followed shortly after with a tap-root, so avoid transplanting from a pot. Seed is best sown directly into the ground.

CZ 9b-10 HZ 1-10

🍃 ☼ ♦◊◊ ↕ 30cm ↔ 20cm ⊙ Jun-Nov

Dichondra

Dichondra repens — This creeping ground cover with small, kidney shaped leaves hugs the ground and is a weed smothering lawn substitute when not exposed to direct sun and excessive heat. In part shade it integrates with pavers elegantly.

CZ 9b-10 HZ 1-7

🍃 ☼☀ ♦♦◊ ↕ 5cm ↔ 10cm

Native Wisteria

Hardenbergia comptoniana — Tiny mauve pea flowers in the hundreds smother this fast growing vine in the toughest conditions.

CZ 9b-10 HZ 1-8

🍃 ☼☀ ♦◊◊ ↕ 3m ↔ 6m ⊙ Aug-Sep

Billy Buttons

Pycnosorus globosus — Butter yellow drumsticks arise from slender, silver foliage throughout spring and summer. Hardly showy, but subtle and suitable for a rock garden.

CZ 9b-10 HZ 1-9

🍃 ☼ ♦◊◊ ↕ 30cm ↔ 15cm ⊙ Nov-Mar

Swan River Daisy

Brachyscome iberidifolia — Precious blue flowers with dark centres (in pink and white colours too) cover narrow leaves. Must have good drainage.

CZ 9b-10 HZ 1-11

🍃 ☼ ♦◊◊ ↕ 40cm ↔ 15cm ⊙ Sep-Nov

> In arid areas with phosphate deficient soils like much of WA, natives will invariably be the first choice for planting. However in richer, fertile soils that support vegetable gardens, fruit and flowers this selection of natives should succeed.

Flannel Flower

Actinotus helianthi — Australia's answer to edelweiss with star shaped flowers and grey foliage. Must have good drainage and moisture at flowering.

CZ 10-11 HZ 1-8

🍃 ☼ ♦♦◊ ↕ 90cm ↔ 45cm ⊙ Sep-Nov

Native Violet

Viola hederacea — Our native violet loves damp shade and spreads somewhat like dichondra. Tiny white flowers and rich blue markings.

CZ 9b-10 HZ 1-7

🍃 ☼☀ ♦♦◊ ↕ 10cm ↔ 30cm ⊙ Sep-Nov

Billy Buttons

Running Postman

Dichondra

Flannel Flower

Native Violet

Native Wisteria

Plants for shade

There are thousands of northern hemisphere plants that thrive in shady areas, however our higher summer temperatures and drier soils restrict the selections. Hellebores and clivias have the showiest flowers and are reliable perennials in the toughest conditions.

Gunnera manicata

Clivia miniata ORANGE

Clivia miniata YELLOW

New Zealand Lily MOUNTAIN BLUE

Chatham Island Forget-Me-Not

New Zealand Lily

Arthropodium cirrhatum — From the New Zealand mountains comes the best evergreen ground cover that survives dry shade and some sun. So much tougher than hostas that snails decimate. Arching, green, strap-like leaves then white flowers appear in spring.

* MOUNTAIN BLUE
  A. milleflorum — An Australian sub-alpine evergreen with elegant blue-grey foliage and white flowers that wave in the breeze.

CZ 9b-11 HZ 1-6

↕ 90cm ↔ 30cm · Nov-Jan

Dodecatheon meadia

Shooting Stars are the American equivalent of hardy cyclamen that appear in spring and retreat underground in summer. Up to a hundred flowers per plant.

CZ 6-10 HZ 1-8

↕ 40cm ↔ 20cm · Oct-Nov

Gunnera manicata

Gigantic 1.5m wide leaves as large as an umbrella can reach 3m tall near boggy soil or running water. As spectacular as *Arum titanium*, with stunning foliage for nine months. Flower cones look prehistoric.

CZ 7-11 HZ 1-7

↕ 3m ↔ 3m · Aug-Sep

Hosta

Hosta sieboldiana — Twelve years of drought have devastated the collections and interest in hostas, but in continually moist shade protected from 35°C days hostas thrive. Literally hundreds of cultivars exist. Needs protection from snails.

CZ 7-11 HZ 1-8

↕ 50cm ↔ 50cm · Nov-Jan

Columbine

Aquilegia sp. — Grannies Bonnets is the common name to describe the nodding flowers that are certainly not old fashioned. Exquisite maidenhair fern-like leaves appeal after flowering. Single or double flowers in white, pink, red, blue, orange and yellow.

* CAMEO PINK & WHITE — White cupped flowers and pink petals. ↕ 40cm ↔ 40cm
* BABY BLUE — Compact plant with bright blue and white flowers. ↕ 40cm ↔ 40cm
* WOODSIDE — Mottled golden foliage with blue flowers. ↕ 20cm ↔ 30cm

CZ 7-11 HZ 1-6 · Sep-Oct

Chatham Island Forget-Me-Not

Myosotidium hortensia — Pleated, dark-green, fleshy leaves support two-tone light and dark-blue forget-me-not flowers. Needs moisture and shade, but the cold salty winds of the roaring forties are like home for it.

CZ 8-11 HZ 1-7

↕ 50cm ↔ 50cm · Sep-Oct

Bergenia cordifolia

Evergreen heart-shaped, deep green leaves form in clumps and tiny pink, white or red flowers appear in spring.

CZ 8-10 HZ 1-8

↕ 20cm ↔ 40cm · Aug-Sep

Clivia miniata

The plant for colour in the shade – particularly dry shade. Dark, evergreen, strap-like leaves and orange, yellow, cream, red or bicolour flowers in spring. Lights up dark areas.

CZ 10-11 HZ 1-7

↕ 40cm ↔ 60cm · Aug-Sep

Dodecatheon meadia

Bergenia cordifolia

Columbine WOODSIDE

Columbine BABY BLUE

Hellebore ASHBOURNE SILVER

Hellebore PINK SPOTTED

Hellebore MIXED

Hellebore DOUBLE PURPLE

Hellebore MIDNIGHT

Hellebores

Major advances in plant breeding have brought the widest selection of Winter Roses for shady areas. They are tough drought survivors and make exquisite bowls of floating blooms indoors.

Helleborous x hybrid VARIETIES

* WHITE — Pure white.
* MIDNIGHT — Purple black single.
* PINK SPOTTED — Pale pink with dark pink spots.

DOUBLE VARIETIES

* DOUBLE PURPLE — Dark purple.
* DOUBLE YELLOW — Pale yellow.
* PICOTEE — Coloured outside edging.

Helleborous sternii VARIETIES

* ASHBOURNE SILVER — Marbled silver leaves.

CZ 8-10 HZ 1-7

🍃 ☀️ 💧💧 ↕ 40cm ↔ 40cm ⊙ Aug-Oct

Himalayan Blue Poppy

Meconopsis grandis — The Holy Grail of flower gardeners comes from Tibet where it colonises meadows that are moist, cool and cloudy overhead. They survive at St Erth if temperatures don't go over 35°C.

CZ 8-9b HZ 1-3

🍃 ☀️ 💧💧💧 ↕ 60cm ↔ 40cm ⊙ Dec

Lily of the Valley

Convallaria majalis — When happy in moist shade and fertile soil this creeping ground cover naturalises with lance shaped foliage and intensely fragrant waxy bells (see p98 for image).

CZ 8-10 HZ 1-7

🍃 ☀️ 💧💧💧 ↕ 15cm ↔ 50cm ⊙ Aug-Sep

Primulas

Primulas provide bursts of colour for moist, shady gardens. Clusters of various colours stand above light green leaves.

* ENGLISH PRIMROSE *Primula vulgaris* — Creamy yellow primroses with a golden eye, sweet fragrance and deeply veined leaves. Multiplies quickly. ↕ 15cm ↔ 15cm
* VICTORIANA GOLD LACE BLACK *Primula x elatior* — Cultivated in the 19th century. Picked flowers last two weeks with sweet fragrance. ↕ 20cm ↔ 20cm
* RED HOT POKER *P. viallii* — Striking "Non-U" colour combination of red and pink is rare in nature. ↕ 30cm ↔ 30cm
* *P. capitata* — Cool violet spinning satellite-like blooms on rich green leaves. ↕ 20cm ↔ 20cm

CZ 8-10 HZ 1-6   🍃 ☀️ 💧💧💧 ⊙ Aug-Sep

Skunk Cabbage

Lysichiton americanus — This iconic marginal water plant has thrived in St Erth's bog garden alongside others like gunnera, primulas, blue poppies and lily of the valley. Perfectly formed yellow arum-like flowers rise one metre, and when happy they colonise large areas.

CZ 8-9b HZ 1-3

🍃 ☀️ 💧💧💧 ↕ 1m ↔ 1.5m ⊙ Oct

Skunk Cabbage

Primula capitata

Primula viallii

Primula GOLD LACE

English Primrose

Himalayan Blue Poppy

Lily of the Valley

Tradescantia Sweet Kate

Bloody Dock

Geranium maderense

Sweet Violets CREPUSCULE

Sweet Violets PRINCESS DE GALLES

Variegated Solomon's Seal

Bloody Dock

Rumex sanguineus — Bloody Dock is an attractive plant with its brightly coloured red veins and striking tongues of green leaves.

CZ 7-10 HZ 1-6

🌣🌑 ♦♦♦ ↕ 30cm ↔ 30cm

Tradescantia Sweet Kate

Tradescantia ohiensis x (subaspera x virginiana) — Bright sunshine collapses most tradescantia foliage and flowers but Sweet Kate's iridescent lime foliage lights up the shade and "shows off" the deep blue flowers. Outstanding selection for a tropical look!

CZ 9a-11 HZ 1-9

🌑 ♦♦♦ ↕ 30cm ↔ 40cm ⊙ Nov-Jan

Geranium maderense

A spectacular flower head 1m across on the most statuesque evergreen pinnate leaved geranium – unlike any other.

- PINK MAGENTA — Pink outer spray with magenta centres.
- WHITE GUERNSEY — White starry flowers and pink centre.

CZ 9-11 HZ 2-12

🌣🌑 ♦♦♦ ↕ 1.2m ↔ 1.5m ⊙ Oct-Nov

Sweet Violets

Viola odorata — Semi-evergreen with underground runners. Needs fertile, well drained, moist soil to produce the sweet perfume. A good coloniser and weed suppressant.

- WHITE PARMA — Double cream on long stems.
- PRINCESS DE GALLES — Huge, single, fragrant mauve blooms.
- CREPUSCULE — Australian selection with single apricot blooms.

CZ 7-10 HZ1-6

🌑 ♦♦♦ ↕ 20cm ↔ 30cm ⊙ Aug-Sep

Variegated Solomon's Seal

Polygonatum falcatum 'Variegata' — Graceful arches of white pendulous flowers tipped with emerald are a joy in semi-shade.

CZ 7-10 HZ 1-7

🌣🌑 ♦♦♦ ↕ 40cm ↔ 40cm ⊙ Sep

Evergreen perennials

Most Australian gardeners live under the mistaken impression that it is our native plants that we must use in our gardens because they survive the climate better. There are two misconceptions here. The first is that a garden can only be created with plants that are exclusive to Australia. 99% of the vegetables and fruits we eat evolved outside Australia.

The second is that Australian plants adapt better to our climate and soils. The biggest collection of native flowers comes from Western Australia and they adapt poorly to soils on the east coast.

Further, the Mediterranean areas of Europe, Western USA, Mexico, Chile and Southern Africa have plant selections ten times as large and more suitable than from WA. Some of our native plants include pre-history fossils like gingko that inhabited Australia before the continents split away.

Evergreen perennials come from these regions having adapted to hot conditions and dry soils (CZ 10 & 11). They are not adapted to extreme cold like herbaceous plants (CZ 8 & 9) but provide foliage cover all year, like flax from New Zealand, geraniums from South Africa or lavender and rosemary from southern France.

Wigandia at Heronswood

Acanthus mollis

This architectural and vigorous plant with huge glossy leaves hold interest all year round, until our extreme 35°C days force a temporary retreat underground for 2 months (Jan-Feb in CZ 10).

Its purple-green spiky flowers in late spring inspired the ancient Greeks to decorate the tops of Corinthian columns.

CZ 7-11 HZ 1-7

 1.2m ↔ 1.5m ◉ Dec-Mar

Agapanthus

This easy-to-grow perennial produces beautiful evergreen shiny, strap-like leaves, vertical flower stems, rounded ball-shaped flowers in blue, purple, white and some with pink blotches.

Unfortunately it is a soloist preferring no competition from other plants. The agapanthus is so tough if left unplanted, will develop roots to find water.

* PURPLE CLOUD *A. inapertus* — Nodding violet-blue. ↕ 1.2m ↔ 60cm

* DWARF WHITE *A. praecox* ↕ 50cm ↔ 40cm

CZ 9b-11 HZ 1-11  ◉ Jan-Feb

Astelia chathamica

From the mountains of New Zealand comes silver sword-like leaves that glisten from a clumping perennial. It stands upright with hidden yellow flowers and orange berries.

Slow growing but easy to divide to spread to other garden parts. Contrasts well with green or bronze in mixed shrub borders.

CZ 9b-10 HZ 1-6

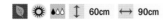 1.2m ↔ 1.2m

Euphorbia

* *E. characias subsp. wulfenii* — This is the lime-green flower that is the best tonic on a glum winters day. Subtle contrasts between flowers and bluish foliage creates pleasing memories.

* *E. characias* 'Silver Swan' — Variegated white edges surround light green leaves before lanterns of white appear.

CZ 9a-10 HZ 1-8

 80cm ↔ 50cm ◉ Jul-Oct

Cyperus papyrus

This Egyptian rush was first used to make paper in pre-biblical days. Whilst a water plant, it is also happy in soils where its structural form is planted *en masse* to highlight its green flowers on stiff stems, not unlike an airy agapanthus.

CZ 9a-12 HZ 1-11

☼ ♦♦◊ ↕ 2m ↔ 2m ◉ All year

Artemisia Powis Castle

A. arborescens — Aromatic, clump forming mound of finely dissected silvery leaves that not only survive but provide elegant accents to green foliage and pastel, plum or blue and yellow colour schemes. Number 1 choice for a border. Woody sub-shrub.

CZ 7-10 HZ 1-7

☼ ♦♦◊ ↕ 60cm ↔ 90cm

Ballota pseudodictamnus

Felted silver-grey leaves are heat absorbing and tough surviving even in poor soils and dry shade. Think of this as a filler, entirely reliable and a plant and forget perennial.

CZ 7-11 HZ 1-8

☼☀ ♦♦◊ ↕ 45cm ↔ 30cm

Ballota

Cyperus papyrus

Euphorbia WULFENII

Euphorbia
SILVER SWAN

Acanthus mollis

Astelia

A. PURPLE CLOUD

Daylily HYPERION

Feathery Bronze Fennel at Heronswood

New Zealand Flax

Daylily STELLA D'ORO

Daylily FULVA FLORE PLENO

Settlers Iris

Algerian Iris

Iris

Iris x hybrid — How do you choose from tens of thousands of cultivars? Modern iris breeders have focused on new breeds when thousands of older varieties are tough, reliable, affordable and have a rare quality – repeat flowers!

SPRING BEARDED VARIETIES

* BEVERLY SILLS — Large ruffled pink. Vigorous, fragrant and repeat flowers. ↕ 85cm ↔ 50cm
* VICTORIA FALLS — Large bright blue ruffled flowers with white flare on the falls. Prolific repeat flowering. ↕ 1m ↔ 60cm
* IMMORTALITY — Pure white repeat flowering. ↕ 70cm ↔ 40cm
* DALMATION IRIS *Iris pallida* 'Variegata' — Pale green leaves with vertical silver stripes and blue, yellow or white flowers. ↕ 1.2m ↔ 50cm
* SETTLERS IRIS *Iris germanica* — Naturalised throughout southern Australian homesteads. These smaller bearded forms thrive in hot dry and even poor soils. ↕ 60m ↔ 30cm

WINTER BEARDLESS VARIETIES

* ALGERIAN IRIS *Iris unguicularis* — A winter delight of massed flowers in white, purple or light blue which we use as edging or for our arid garden. ↕ 40cm ↔ 30cm ☉ Jun-Sep

CZ 8-10 HZ 1-8 Nov-Dec

Bronze Fennel

Foeniculum vulgare — Self supporting and aromatic with plumes of bronzy feathers are an outstanding foliage contrast to more solid shrubs. Anise scented fennel leaves are perfect for fish. Cut the yellow flowers off to avoid re-seeding.

CZ 7-10 HZ 1-8

 ↕ 1.5m ↔ 40cm ☉ Nov-Dec

Daylilies

Hemerocallis sp. — Flowers open and close in a day but provide continuous flowering through the season in yellow, white, purple, pink, bronze and bicolours – over 30,000 named cultivars! Flowers are edible and form from clumping fleshy foliage tough enough to be used on freeway verges in the USA.

* HYPERION — Extremely fragrant canary yellow single flowers from deciduous leaves. ↕ 1m ↔ 40cm
* *H. fulva* 'Flore Pleno' — Double burnt-orange 15cm flowers with a red eye on deciduous leaves. ↕ 75cm ↔ 50cm
* CORKY — Bright lemon flowers with brown backs on deciduous foliage. ↕ 85cm ↔ 40cm
* STELLA D'ORO — Open golden flowers 6cm across are vigorous and continuous. Good for pots. ↕ 30cm ↔ 30cm

CZ 7-12 HZ 1-9  Oct-Mar

New Zealand Flax

Phormium tenax — The flax and paving phase that swept suburbia created *'survivable rather than desirable gardens'*. Lacking shade, greenery or food plants they are an abomination. But the monarch of all accent plants is the purple, sword-like leaves of New Zealand flax.

CZ9b-11 HZ 1-8

↕ 2m ↔ 1.5m

Three groups of plants

TO BE AVOIDED
Bedding plants for beginners only.

SURVIVORS BUT UNDESIRABLE
Flax, diosma and nandina.

HIGHLY DESIRABLE
Original wildflowers, perennials, shrub roses and rainforest evergreen trees.

Pink Statice

Red Hot Pokers PERCY'S PRIDE

Red Hot Pokers

Kniphofia sp. — Red hot pokers can look warming and uplifting on a cold winter's day but oppressive in the hot Australian sun. Hence our *not so red* hot selections!

* BORDER BALLET — Dwarf and delicate flower spikes, yellow orange above grass-like leaves.
* PERCY'S PRIDE — Lime green summer spikes are refreshing like, *Euphorbia wulfenii* in early spring.

CZ 7-10 HZ 1-8
🍃 ☀ 💧 ↕ 60cm ↔ 60cm ⚙ Nov-Feb

Pelargonium

Commonly called geraniums, pelargoniums hail from southern Africa. The wonderful foliage is aromatic, evergreen and highly desirable. Will not survive frost but thrives in hot dry conditions. Best markings in cooler months.

* CHOC-MINT GERANIUM — Large dark green leaves with charcoal oak leaf marking.
* LADY PLYMOUTH — White variegated edging of pale green crumpled leaves gives light contrast.
* SNOWFLAKE — White markings on mid-green, like flecks of snow.

CZ 10-11 HZ 3-8
🍃 ☀ 💧 ↕ 60cm ↔ 60cm ⚙ Oct-Dec

Lavender Cotton

Santolina chamaecyparissus — With the smell of the sea on clean sheets, lavender cotton evokes the sun and grey foliage of lavender. Silver, almost white, woolly shoots are covered with pale yellow buttons.

* MINORCAN *S. magonica* — Aromatic, carpeting form. ↕ 30m ↔ 60cm

CZ 8-10 HZ 2-10
🍃 ☀ 💧 ↕ 50cm ↔ 50cm ⚙ Oct-Dec

Pink Statice

Limonium peregrinum — Rare perennial statice that still looks good in a vase 4-5 *years* later. Pink sprays are truly everlasting on the bush. Thrives in hot dry coastal and sandy conditions. Green paddles of leathery green foliage.

CZ 9b-11 HZ 3-9
🍃 ☀ 💧 ↕ 60cm ↔ 60cm ⚙ Nov-Apr

Lavender

Lavandula angustifolia — It's not just the perfume and the cool blue colour, it's the nectar for bees and the evergreen, fine, felty-grey leaves so successful for hedging. Drought tolerant and ideal for coastal, even sandy and salty gardens.

* ENGLISH LAVENDER — Blue or white. ↕ 1m ↔ 1m
* MUNSTEAD — Blue purple flowers on a compact plant. ↕ 45cm ↔ 40cm
* DWARF FRENCH MONET *L. dentata* — Elegant form with repeat flowering and some shade tolerance. ↕ 50m ↔ 40cm
* *L x intermedia* 'Grosso' — The blue cultivar for perfume. ↕ 70m ↔ 40cm

CZ 7-10 HZ 1-8
🍃 ☀ 💧 ⚙ Dec-Jan

Rosemary

Rosmarinus officinalis — Aromatic culinary woody shrub that makes an outstanding hedge, ground cover or wall hanging with blue flowers that should be preferred to lavender because it's so tough in both dry and humid summers. Pink and white flower forms available.

* TUSCAN BLUE — Fast growing, vigorous and tall with deep blue flowers. ↕ 1m ↔ 80cm
* HANGING ROSEMARY *R. prostratus* — One of the most memorable garden images at Heronswood. ↕ 50cm ↔ 70cm

CZ 8-11 HZ 1-10
🍃 ☀ 💧 ⚙ Jun-Oct

Purple Tradescantia

Tradescantia pallida 'Purple Haze' — It looks somewhat out of place until it gets hot and then the combination of cannas, bananas, daylilies and alstroemerias give it 'the tropical look' that seems just right!

CZ 9a-11 HZ 4-9
🍃 ☀ 💧 ↕ 30cm ↔ 1m ⚙ Dec-Feb

Purple Tradescantia

Lavender with Lavender Cotton at Killara

Hanging Rosemary

Rosemary

Pelargonium
SNOW FLAKE

Pelargonium
CHOC-MINT GERANIUM

English Lavender

Succulents

Yucca desmetiana

Senecio serpens

Agave Nova

Echeveria BLACK PRINCE

Aeonium Schwartzkopf VELOUR

Cotyledon SILVER WAVES

Succulents create form and shape in the garden

Echeveria sp.

Is there any more beautifully constructed plant for rockeries, pots and bowls? These gems thrive in the sun with little water.

CZ 9a-11 HZ 1-7

☼ ⚬⚬⚬ ↕ 20cm ↔ 25cm

Senecio serpens

With its appealing stubby jellybean-like leaves, this ground cover is one of the most valuable landscaping succulents. Its light blue stumps brighten dark and shady areas all year, whilst holding fluffy cream flowers in summer.

CZ 9a-11 HZ 1-9

☼ ⚬⚬⚬ ↕ 15cm ↔ 60cm ◉ Nov-Jan

Kalanchoe beharensis

Is it a sculpture or a pet? With a thick rust coloured pelt that begs to be stroked. Grows tall in time and needs no water or special fertiliser.

CZ 10-11 HZ 1-10

☼ ⚬⚬⚬ ↕ 2m ↔ 1m

Cotyledon Silver Waves

Cotyledon orbiculata — Powdery silver-white wavy leaves cope with sun or shade as well as dry and stony soils.

CZ 9b-11 HZ 1-8

☼☼ ⚬⚬⚬ ↕ 30cm ↔ 30cm

Echeveria VIOLET QUEEN

Aeonium

* SCHWARTZKOPF — Tightly packed rosettes of black are striking before bright yellow flowers. Almost indestructible statues.
  ↕ 1m ↔ 1m

* VELOUR — More-compact rosettes retain green centres without forming a trunk.
  ↕ 50cm ↔ 1m

CZ 9-11 HZ 4-9

☼ ⚬⚬⚬ ◉ Sep-Nov

Yucca desmetiana

At the exquisitely designed volcano at Melbourne's botanic garden this is one of the selections that will take your breath away. Dusky pink fleshy rosettes have a vertical stature.

CZ 9b-12 HZ 2-14

☼ ⚬ ↕ 1.2m ↔ 60cm ◉ Nov-Feb

Opuntia Burbank Spineless

O. ficus-indica — Did Dr. Seuss create this plant with no leaves, branches or anything green? Red edible fruit appear on pads that are spineless, thanks to a breeding breakthrough developed by the nineteenth century Californian pioneer in agricultural science, Luther Burbank.

CZ 10-12 HZ 1-11

☼ ⚬⚬⚬ ↕ 2m ↔ 1m

Agave attenuata

Stunning feature plant with magnificent fleshy, grey-green rosettes that give rise to 2m tall flower spikes after 4-5 years. This is the most attention seeking and deserving textural plant.

* NOVA — Beautiful light blue.

CZ 9b-11 HZ 1-11

☼ ⚬⚬⚬ ↕ 1m ↔ 1.5m

Grasses

Elegia capensis

As elegant and precise as a Japanese tea ceremony, the purplish bracts unfurl on green stems then tufts of green vertical rush-like leaves appear creating an intriguing display over two months. Must have wet soil.

CZ 9b-12 HZ 1-6

 ☀ ▲▲▲ ↕ 1.5m ↔ 60cm

Stipa gigantea

Intriguing and subtle copper-gold flowers and slender stems that sway gently in the breeze. It's a real feature in Heronswood's border.

CZ 7-11 HZ 1-8

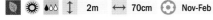 ☀ ▲◊◊ ↕ 2m ↔ 70cm ◉ Nov-Feb

Mondo Grass

- *Ophiopogon japonicus* — Tufted mounds provide lawn replacements of grass-like foliage with little water.
- BLACK *O. planiscapus* 'Nigrescens' — Black grass that looks startling next to pebbles.

CZ 7-11 HZ 1-8

 ☀☀ ▲▲◊ ↕ 20cm ↔ 30cm

Fountain Grass

Pennisetum setaceum — The display on the edge of our duck pond starts in December and remains in flower until April. Beautiful pinkish grey plumes. Easy and drought tolerant.

- BURGUNDY GIANT — Purple red leaves.
- FEATHERTOP GRASS *P. villosum* — Creamy white heads.

CZ 9b-12 HZ 1-8

 ☀ ▲◊◊ ↕ 1.2m ↔ 80cm ◉ Dec-Apr

Miscanthus

- *Miscanthus sinensis* 'Variegatus' — Vaulting pale green leaves with cream and white margins followed in autumn by silky pink flower heads turning to straw in winter.
- *M. sinensis* 'Zebrinus' — Horizontal bands of creamy white.
- *M. x giganteus* — Bio-fuel, producing 12 tonnes of dry matter per acre, twice that of corn. This is a serious carbon sequestration plant with potential to replace fossil fuel energy for coal fired power. In the garden it is a fast growing screen or back of border plant. Sterile. Life span is 15-30 years.

CZ 8-11 HZ 1-6

 ☀ ▲▲◊ ↕ 4m ↔ 2m ◉ Feb-Apr

"Always remember it is the least drought tolerant plants that determine how much water should be given to a garden border."
JAMES HITCHMOUGH

Fountain Grass

Fountain Grass BURGUNDY GIANT

Mondo Grass

Mondo Grass BLACK

Stipa gigantea

Elegia capensis

Miscanthus Variegatus

Early flowering perennials

Geranium ROZANNE

Foxglove PAM'S SPLIT

Foxglove GLITTERING PRIZES

Clary Sage VATICAN WHITE

Campanula persicifolia

Anthemis EC BUXTON

Catmint

Nepeta x fassenii — With loose, airy foliage (that cats adore), catmint echoes the attributes of lavender; with grey, aromatic foliage and violet blue or white flowers that bees love but without the stiff woody stems. Indispensable as a long flowering ground cover under roses or combine with pink evening primrose. Tough and heat loving.

* WALKERS LOW — Front of border.
  ↕ 30cm ↔ 30cm
* WHITE — Outstanding groundcover.
  ↕ 30cm ↔ 30cm
* SIX HILLS GIANT — Vigorous growth and tall stems. ↕ 90cm ↔ 50cm
* GIANT CATMINT *N. tuberosa* — Purple vertical spikes. ↕ 80cm ↔ 50cm

CZ 7-10 HZ 1-10
↕ 30cm ↔ 30m Sep-Mar

Russell Lupin

Lupinus polyphyllus — One of the most exciting breeding breakthroughs last century. George Russell, starting with the blue *L. hartwegii*, planted thousands of plants from different species over 25 years to offer every colour and bicolour. The first choice perennial in a cottage garden, a rose garden or wildflower verge like we have done at St Erth. Prefers acid soil, no manures and frost. Also a nitrogen fixing plant.

CZ 7-10 HZ 1-6
↕ 1.2m ↔ 45cm Dec-Jan

Campanula persicifolia

Commonly called Canterbury Bells, with dense rosettes of peach-like foliage provide magical, pendulous bell shaped flowers. Must have frost.

CZ 7-9b HZ 1-7
↕ 90cm ↔ 30cm Oct-Nov

Clary Sage Vatican White

Salvia sclarea — This woolly, grey leaved salvia rises to spectacular heights in just 3 months with elegant towers of pure white flower bracts. Although a biennial, like foxglove, it is well worth planting.

CZ 7-10 HZ 1-10
↕ 1.2m ↔ 80cm Dec-Feb

Geranium Rozanne

G himalaense x wallichianum — Tough and desirable. Bright blue flowers for 4 months through the heat of summer. Dark green, marbled foliage that forms a neat ground covering.

CZ 7-10 HZ 1-6
↕ 40cm ↔ 50cm Oct-Apr

Anthemis EC Buxton

A. tinctoria — Hundreds of showy lemon-yellow daisies with orange centres cover ferny green, aromatic foliage that hugs the ground.

CZ 7-10 HZ 1-10
↕ 60cm ↔ 80cm Nov-Feb

Foxglove

Digitalis purpurea — Whilst there are many perennial foxgloves in bronze, yellow or pink colours, none are as showy as the thimbles of spotted, hanging flowers reaching 2m tall in spring. Although biennial, provided it is planted before winter, it is a magical sight in a cottage or shady garden.

* PAM'S SPLIT — Ruffled spikes with split corollas.
* GLITTERING PRIZES — Pinks, purples and whites with delicate spots.

CZ 7-10 HZ 1-6
↕ 2m ↔ 40cm Oct-Nov

Sea Lavender

Valerian

Wallflower WINTER JOY

Russell Lupin

True Pyrethrum

Tanacetum cinerariifolium — Commercially grown in Tasmania, the flowers are harvested as a natural insecticide. Delicate grey ferny foliage and masses of floppy, pure white flowers look fetching hanging over a wall, pot or in a herb garden.

CZ 7-10 HZ 1-9

☀ ⬡⬡ ↕ 40cm ↔ 30cm ⊙ Nov-Mar

Oriental Poppy

Papaver orientale — Is this the most voluptuous flower? Huge, crepe-like, textural, breakfast bowl-sized flowers expose a central disk of black stamens bees get in a frenzy for. Spectacular flowering is short but unforgettable. Combine with lupins for a classic vertical/globular contrast as we do at St Erth. Must have frost.

- BEAUTY OF LIVERMERE — Glazed red.
- CHOIR BOY — White, pleated petals.

CZ 7-9b HZ 1-6

☀ ⬡⬡ ↕ 1m ↔ 30cm ⊙ Dec-Jan

Shasta Shaggy Gem

Leucanthemum x superbum — A summer favourite. Use this pure white daisy with its curved and fringed 12cm flowers to combine with blue agapanthus. Cut back for an autumn flowering.

CZ 7-10 HZ 1-9

☀ ⬡⬡⬡ ↕ 90cm ↔ 50cm ⊙ Dec-Feb

Wallflower Winter Joy

Erysimum — A true perennial wallflower selected in New Zealand for its fragrance, colour and perennial performance. Mauve-purple flowers repeat if dead headed.

CZ 7-10 HZ 1-9

☀☀ ⬡⬡ ↕ 70cm ↔ 70cm ⊙ Aug-Oct

Cottage gardeners

Use early season perennials and hardy annuals like Californian poppies, hollyhocks and sweet peas (see page 145 & 148) under fruit trees and roses to create a cheerfully disordered spring display.

Sea Lavender

Limonium perezii — Purple-blue statice flowers last forever above leathery and evergreen leaves. Thrives in salty, sandy and hot conditions and combines well with valerian.

CZ 9a-11 HZ 1-10

☀ ⬡⬡ ↕ 70cm ↔ 40cm ⊙ All year

Meadow Sage Blue Hills

Salvia x sylvestris — This mid-blue border salvia will flower up to 3 times after being cut back, making it a spectacular mainstay in any flower garden. Compact and drought tolerant.

CZ 8-10 HZ 1-10

☀ ⬡⬡⬡ ↕ 40cm ↔ 40cm ⊙ Dec-Apr

Valerian

Centranthus ruber — In Monet's Garden at Giverny, bearded iris combine with valerian and this magnificent match is copied throughout France. More showy than the herb valerian, it hangs from walls and repeats without dead heading. Available in white and pink.

CZ 7-10 HZ 1-7

☀☀ ⬡⬡ ↕ 80cm ↔ 50cm ⊙ Oct-Feb

Oriental Poppy CHOIR BOY

Meadow Sage BLUE HILLS

True Pyrethrum

Shasta SHAGGY GEM

Late flowering perennials SUMMER & AUTUMN

Angelica EBONY SUPERIOR

Achillea TERRACOTTA

Achillea MOONSHINE

Agastache BLUE FORTUNE

Aster MONCH

JAPANESE WINDFLOWER

Agastache APRICOT SPRITE

Aster Monch

Aster x frikartii — Classic autumn flowers combine with golden rod and *Helenium* to brighten cooler autumn days. Light blue daisies that flower twice as long, don't fall over and are disease free compared to hundreds of other asters.

CZ 8-10 HZ 1-8

🍃 ☀️☀️ 💧💧💧 ↕ 60cm ↔ 40m ◉ Feb-Apr

Agastache

Some of the best 'new' plants in 20 years, these outstanding long flowering perennials from the mint family soak up the heat, provide pleasing aromas and tubular flowers that birds seek for nectar. Longer flowering than any annuals.

VERTICAL FLOWERS

• BLUE FORTUNE — Powder-blue liquorice scented flowers last for months. Contrast elegantly with coneflowers and achilleas. Vertical flowers of the Hummingbird Mint have citronella scented leaves.

BICOLOUR, AIRY FORMS

• AZTEC ROSE *A. mexicana* — Densely packed vibrant pink.
• LEMON FIESTA — Intriguing dark purple bracts open to lemon, Hummingbird Mint tubular flowers.
• APRICOT SPRITE *A. aurantiaca* — Compact apricot flowers are striking against purple bracts.

CZ 8-10 HZ 1-10

🍃 ☀️ 💧💧💧 ↕ 1m ↔ 50cm ◉ Dec-Apr

A well grown perennial can produce 10 times as many flowers as one poorly grown, providing soil is fertile and mulched in spring.

Japanese Windflower

Anemone scabiosa — The first choice to brighten up the shade when summer finishes. Deep green, three fingered leaves smother the weeds and provide exquisite pure white or pink anemone-like flowers in autumn. Needs moist soil and shelter from wind.

CZ 7-10 HZ 1-7

🍃 ☀️ 💧💧💧 ↕ 1.2m ↔ 1m ◉ Mar-May

Achillea

Also known as Yarrow, these flat topped ferny foliage flowers have a see-through quality and a horizontal flowering plane that contrasts beautifully with clumping and vertical shapes.

The mainstay of the most memorable summer borders. Cut back to induce repeat flowering.

• *A. clypeolata* — Compact golden yellow rays with divided silver leaves.
  ↕ 20cm ↔ 50cm

• HELLA GLASSHOFF — An almost iridescent, flat topped, moonshine lemon-yellow. Well behaved clumping alternative to *A. taygeta* 'Moonshine'. ↕ 50cm ↔ 50cm

• TERRACOTTA — Opening orange, fading to yellow. Contrasts beautifully with delphinium Blue Sensation.
  ↕ 80cm ↔ 60cm

CZ 7-10 HZ 1-10

🍃 ☀️ 💧💧💧 ◉ Nov-Feb

Angelica Ebony Superior

Angelica sylvestris — A sight to behold reaching 2m in a Californian garden we visited. Fast growing, near black stems provide the scaffolding for masses of purple-pink flower umbels. Shelter from hot, dry conditions.

CZ 7-10 HZ 1-6

🍃 ☀️☀️ 💧💧💧 ↕ 1.5m ↔ 50cm ◉ Nov-Feb

106

Sea Holly BLUE STAR

Hollyhock HALO MIXED

Delphinium BLUE SENSATION

Sea Holly

Eryngium sp. — Heat lovers from dry, rocky soils with masses of cylindrical flowers displayed above conspicuous bracts, distinguishing them from globe thistles. With moisture seeking taproots they are as tough as they are beautiful. Outstanding cut or dried flowers.

- MISS WILLMOTT'S GHOST *E. giganteum* — Exquisite, jewel-like cones sit above silvery ghost-like bracts as if touched by the full moon. Easily grown biennial.
  ↕ 1m ↔ 50cm

- BLUE STAR *E. alpinum* — Metallic blue bracts almost clasp a black, fir-like cone.
  ↕ 80cm ↔ 50cm

CZ 7-10 HZ 1-8 Dec-Jan

Hollyhock

Alcea rosea — Is there any plant more widely abused? The plant breeders have taken an elegant unassuming cottager's plant that reached perfection and dwarfed it, *transforming its simplicity into a garish double powder puff.* Long flowering in a sunny position, best planted singly to avoid spread of rust.

- HALO SERIES — Thankfully the cheerful 2m high, unsophisticated, single flowering is back but with the two tone halo series. 10-15cm flowers with central contrasting violet black eye or golden chartreuse halo. Available in white, yellow, pink, red and purple colours.

CZ 7-10 HZ 1-8
  ↕ 2m ↔ 60cm ⊙ Dec-Mar

Delphinium

To walk among the alpine meadows of Yosemite and see masses of lupins and delphiniums growing wild is unforgettable. Modern breeding has created 2m tall columns and dwarf forms that make breathtaking pictures. Must have fertile well drained soil.

- BLUE SENSATION — Unforgettable gentian blue flowers keep coming from a much branched healthy bush without staking. Discovered in NZ, it is our no.1 perennial, and being sterile keeps flowering when cut back. Pink available. ↕ 1m ↔ 50cm

- PACIFIC GIANTS — Bred in California to cope with heat stress these spectacular columns would be the no.1 choice at a wedding or for the back of the border. 2m high plants need wind protection and staking. White, light and dark blue, black, purple and lilac, all but yellow and red colours. Flower spikes are up to 1.3m with up to 100 florets. ↕ 2m ↔ 80cm

- BELLADONNA — Compact, short spikes reach 60-90cm tall producing single flowers of blue, white and violet. ↕ 1m ↔ 50cm

CZ 7-10 HZ 1-6 Nov-Feb

Inula magnifica

This giant of a perennial has flat daisy-like flowers of golden yellow and ascends to nearly 2m from a long living clump in just three months at St Erth. Tolerates shade and wet soils and suits naturalised woodland.

CZ 7-10 HZ 1-6
 ↕ 1.8m ↔ 1m ⊙ Jan-Feb

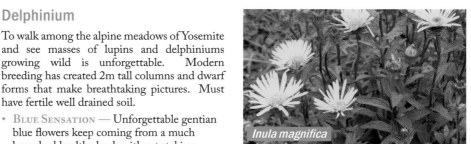

Inula magnifica

Sea Holly MISS WILLMOTT'S GHOST

Delphinium PACIFIC GIANTS

The most popular cut flowers, such as carnations, gladiolus and hybrid tea roses do not make attractive garden displays. But if you choose delphiniums, coneflowers, eryngiums and achilleas, you can have the best of both worlds.

Coneflower SUNRISE

Coneflower TIKI TORCH

Echinops Globe Flower VEITCH'S BLUE

Coneflower MAGNUS SUPERIOR

Coneflower HAPPY STAR

Crocosmia SOLFATARE

Cardoon

Crocosmia LUCIFER

Gaillardia ARIZONA SUN

Cardoon

Cynara cardunculus — Selection from the statuesque edible artichoke we use to great effect at Heronswood. Up to 1.8m tall deep cut spiky grey leaves that look like a permanent sculpture before it provides 32 or 64 huge purple thistle-like flowers. Evergreen sun lover.

CZ 7-10 HZ 1-9

 ☀ ♦♦♦ ↕ 1.8m ↔ 80cm ⊙ Sep-Oct

Crocosmia

Montbretia, which is a weedy relative, has none of the stature and form of these lance shaped leaves forming clumps then showy branches of colour. Multiplies easily as it's a set and forget corm.

- SOLFATARE — Bronze leaves contrast apricot yellow blooms to subdue the brightness of hot yellows. ↕ 60cm ↔ 50cm
- LUCIFER — Tomato red arching flowers on branched spikes. A must for a hot border. ↕ 1m ↔ 60cm

CZ 8-11 HZ 1-8 ☀ ♦♦♦ ⊙ Jan-Mar

Echinops Globe Thistle

These globe thistles stand proud with sturdy stems and thistle-like spiky leaves with grey undersides. Tough, drought tolerant plants, make good cut flowers, fresh or dried, and are a magnet for bees.

- STAR FROST *E. bannaticus* — White globe thistle.
- VEITCH'S BLUE *E. ritro* — As striking and in the same league as Blue Sensation delphinium, the metallic blue flower is small but there are masses of them. Excellent repeat flowering.

CZ 7-10 HZ 1-6

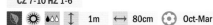 ☀ ♦♦♦ ↕ 1m ↔ 80cm ⊙ Oct-Mar

Coneflower

Echinacea purpurea — From this popular herb a huge breeding effort has created entirely new colours to the ultimate summer perennial.

The flat flower has horizontal petals that after pollination creates a dark cone. The petals reflex down leaving and attractive dark seed head

This 3 dimensional plant flowers for months. A fragrant cut flower which must have a good moist soil.

- MAGNUS SUPERIOR — Reddish-pink petals with dark centres.
- HAPPY STAR — Soundly perennial, with white petals and green cone.
- TIKI TORCH — Bright orange petals, red-tinged cone.
- SUNRISE — Pale yellow petals, greenish-orange cone.

CZ 7-11 HZ 1-10

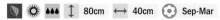 ☀ ♦♦♦ ↕ 80cm ↔ 40cm ⊙ Sep-Mar

Gaillardia Blanket Flower

Gaillardia x grandiflora — A perennial for hot, dry conditions that produces masses of bright flowers that can look tiring on a hot day. Our selections, in appealing colours, flower well into autumn when the warm weather recedes.

- BURGUNDY — Double flowered, deep wine-red. ↕ 50cm ↔ 50cm
- ARIZONA SUN — Appealing apricot colour with touches of red in the centre. ↕ 30cm ↔ 30cm

CZ 7-10 HZ 1-6 ☀ ♦♦♦ ⊙ Sep-Mar

Dahlia BISHOP OF LLANDAFF

Arrowroot

Canna STUTTGART

Canna BENGAL TIGER

Dahlia BISHOP OF DOVER

Coreopsis

Bright and sunny flowers with unsophisticated daisy form that last through summer. New hybrids with airy stems create masses of flowers like the perennial equivalent of annual bedding plants. Suitable for pots and balconies.

- MOONBEAM *C. verticulata* — Sulphur yellow flowers for months in garden beds. ↕ 40cm ↔ 30cm
- LIMEROCK RUBY *C. rosea* — Bright ruby red repeat well when cut back. ↕ 40cm ↔ 60cm
- SNOWBERRY *C. auriculata* — Striking three tone petals with berry disk and yellow centre. ↕ 50cm ↔ 50cm

CZ 7-10 HZ 1-10 Dec-Feb

Canna

Canna x generalis — Described by one wit as 'gladiolus gone bananas' which explains the tropical look of the leaves. Thriving in hot or dry and the humid tropics the orange striped foliage can look oppressive in hot dry southern gardens but appeal in the overcast tropics.

- BENGAL TIGER Variegated thin green stripes on lime create the cool tropical look followed by large orange flowers.
- PANACHE — Delicate apricot flowers for the back of the border.
- STUTTGART — For those who want 'cool leafed cannas' irregular green and white panels. Small orange flowers.
- ARROWROOT *C. indica edulis* — An elegant edible we discovered in a Vietnamese community garden. Mid-green leaves with thin purple veins and edging. Used in stir-fries but an excellent foliage plant too.

CZ 7-10 HZ 1-10

 ↕ 2m ↔ 75cm Dec-Apr

Alstroemeria

Alstroemeria sp. — Known as Peruvian Lily, this is one of the best bulbs for a summer flower garden wearing yellow petals that contain short, marked lines. Easy to grow and vigorous, pluck the stems from the base for great cut flowers.

- WHITE — With yellow upper petals.
- PEACH MELBA — Yellow with pink markings.

CZ 8-11 HZ 1-11

 ↕ 80cm ↔ 50cm Oct-Mar

Dahlia

Over 20,000 cultivars exist but 95% of them have double, top heavy flowers that unbalance the plant and need staking. However, the single flowered forms are invaluable providing five months of colour. Bulbs (tubers) need lifting in heavy frost prone areas.

- BISHOP OF LLANDAFF — A 1920s re-discovery with electric scarlet semi-double flowers offset by bronze foliage creating the number 1 flower for a 'hot border'. Combine with canna Bengal Tiger for the tropical look. ↕ 1m ↔ 60cm
- BISHOP OF DOVER — Single white with yellow centre on dark stems and leaves. ↕ 1m ↔ 60cm
- LE COCO — Bronze foliage companion of the Bishop with bright yellow single flowers with a central ring of red. ↕ 1.2m ↔ 60cm
- CAFÉ AU LAIT — Decorative double that's all the rage in the wedding scene. Needs staking. ↕ 1.2m ↔ 60cm
- TREE DAHLIA *D. imperalis* — The Jack and the Beanstalk version reaching 3-4m in late autumn. Single or double flowers in lilac, pink or white. Huge bulbs should be planted behind wind protecting shrubs to provide 'upper circle' display. Cut to the ground in winter. ↕ 3-4m ↔ 1m ☉ Apr-May

CZ 9b-11 HZ 1-11 Nov-Apr

Alstroemeria WHITE

Alstroemeria YELLOW

Coreopsis SNOWBERRY

Coreopsis LIMEROCK RUBY

Gypsophila paniculata

Penstemon ELECTRIC BLUE

Penstemon SOUR GRAPES

Scabiosa Pincushion

Rudbeckia Goldsturn

Phlox BLUE PARADISE

Californian Tree Poppy

Romneya coulteri — A signature Diggers favourite, once seen, never forgotten. Huge bowls of white crepe paper scented flowers with a pompom of golden stamens. Arching sprays of grey produce hundreds of flowers in hot dry areas. Hates root disturbance but can be invasive. Heronswood has a 31 year old plant!

CZ 7-10 HZ 1-10

 ☀ ●◊◊ ↕ 2m ↔ 3m ◉ Dec-Apr

Whirling Butterflies

Gaura lindheimeri — An American prairie wildflower now so common as to question its place in the discerning garden, but surely any permanent perennial is better than annuals or potted colour. Clouds of pink or white butterflies suit the natural areas of a garden.

CZ 7-10 HZ 1-10

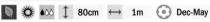 ☀ ●◊◊ ↕ 80cm ↔ 1m ◉ Dec-May

Phlox paniculata

Dame Elizabeth Murdoch's walled garden utilizes phlox in all its traditional glory, with whites and pinks to provide a foreground to delphiniums and dahlias. Sadly, too few gardeners enjoy these fragrant coin-like flowers.

• BLUE PARADISE — Medium blue flowers with dark eyes. Are there ever enough cool blue flowers in summer?

CZ 7-10 HZ 1-7

 ☀ ●◊◊ ↕ 90cm ↔ 70cm ◉ Dec-Feb

Gypsophila paniculata

Baby's Breath describes the airy mound of white flowers that florists use to accentuate more striking flower arrangements. It is a tap rooted tough border perennial that can fill in gaps left by spring bulbs or oriental poppies. Apply calcium to facilitate vigorous flowering.

• BRISTOL FAIRY — Outstanding double flowers for a white garden.

CZ 7-10 HZ 3-8

 ☀ ●◊◊ ↕ 90cm ↔ 1m ◉ Dec-Feb

Gaura WHIRLING BUTTERFLIES

Penstemon

With tubular summer flowers but evergreen foliage this is a perennial form of short foxglove, or snapdragon. 25cm heads of tubular flower comes in all colours but yellow.

• SWAN LAKE — Classic serene white.
  ↕ 60cm ↔ 40cm
• SOUR GRAPES — Like bunches of flowers of deep mauve with a white throat.
  ↕ 60cm ↔ 40cm
• ELECTRIC BLUE *P. x heterophyllus* — Age to neon pink. ↕ 50cm ↔ 60cm

CZ 9-11 HZ 1-9

 ☀ ●◊◊ ◉ Dec-Mar

Scabiosa Pincushion

Scabiosa caucasica 'Blue' — Flowers that last all summer in lavender-blue and white colours. A highly sought after cut flower, that also harmonises well in yellow colour schemes in summer borders.

CZ 7-10 HZ 3-8

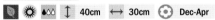 ☀ ●◊◊ ↕ 40cm ↔ 30cm ◉ Dec-Apr

Rudbeckia Goldsturn

Rudbeckia fulgida — Black Eyed Susans are from American prairies. With smaller cones than coneflowers and usually yellow petals, they look comfortable with their horizontal flowers contrasting with straw coloured vertical grasses popularised by James van Sweden. Excellent perennial to light up an autumn garden, or as a foreground to Russian sage.

CZ 7-10 HZ 1-7

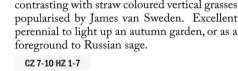 ☀ ●◊◊ ↕ 60cm ↔ 40cm ◉ Feb-Mar

Perennials for the seaside

Many perennials will thrive in hot, dry, sandy soils provided you select those with drought tolerance. Gardens by the sea can enjoy a colourful summer by choosing agapanthus, baby's tears, dianthus, marjoram, lavender, geraniums, curry plant, rosemary, salvias, pink statice, sea lavender and thyme.

Californian Tree Poppy

Russian Sage

Perovskia atriplicifolia — A mainstay of a summer perennial garden providing powder-blue tall flower panicles from deeply grey leaves. This is lavender-like in colour and tone but its airy flower form works with neighbours unlike the stiff wood-like lavender.

CZ 7-10 HZ 1-10

 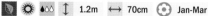 1.2m ↔ 70cm 🔆 Jan-Mar

Salvia

Salvias have become popular because of their drought tolerance but just surviving is no justification for "garden worthiness".

Most shrubby salvias flower in autumn and winter, and summer flowering salvias mostly have flowers that are arid looking, too small or sparsely spaced. We recommend:

SUMMER FLOWERS 🔆 Sep-Jan

- PURPLE RAIN *S. verticulata* — A repeat flowering salvia with deep purple flowers. ↕ 40cm ↔ 70cm

- PURPLE MAJESTY *S. guarantica* — A tall back-of-border perennial with purple flowers with black calyx. ↕ 1.5m ↔ 1m

- INDIGO SPIRES *S. farinacea* — A violet covered perennial stem similar to the annual blue salvia. ↕ 1.2m ↔ 1m

AUTUMN FLOWERS 🔆 Jan-May

- *S. azurea* — Clear blue flowers smother the plant. Its lax habit suits less formal garden areas. ↕ 50cm ↔ 80cm

- MEXICAN SAGE *S. leucantha* — This velvet sage is tactile, like a blanket of grey. Available in white, pink and purple forms. ↕ 1.2m ↔ 1m

- ANTHONY PARKER *S. leucantha x elegans* — Perfectly shaped mounding shrub with short purple-blue spikes that flower for months in autumn. ↕ 1m ↔ 1m

CZ 7-10 HZ 1-10

   80cm ↔ 40m

Russian Sage

Mexican Sage

Salvia ANTHONY PARKER

Salvia INDIGO SPIRES with *Achillea clypeolata*

Salvia PINK VELOUR

Salvia PURPLE MAJESTY

Salvia PURPLE RAIN

Verbascum BANANA CUSTARD

Sedum AUTUMN JOY

Verbena bonariensis

Verbascum SOUTHERN CHARM

Verbascum OLYMPICUM

Verbascum

Commonly called Mullein, these exclamation marks on a horizontal plane are indispensable vertical focal points, like percussion is to an orchestra. Tolerant of poor soils, dry conditions and neglect.

- SOUTHERN CHARM — White coin-like open flowers with a purple eye. ↕ 1m ↔ 40cm
- BANANA CUSTARD — Two tone yellow flowers on woolly stems. ↕ 2m ↔ 40cm
- *V. olympicum* — Branching stems carry yellow or white tall and broad flower spikes. ↕ 2m ↔ 1m

CZ 9a-10 HZ 1-10   Dec-Feb

Lamb's Ears

Stachys byzantina — So furry it feels more like the cat you want to stroke. This could be described as the ultimate perennial. Soft, felty tactile leaves are intensely beautiful before short stems of tiny, subtle, pink flowers rise. Its grey foliage contrasts beautifully with green so it's a 3-dimensional garden-worthy plant that should be in each garden.

- BIG EARS — A somewhat coarser leaf with irregular flower spikes that takes even more heat and dryness.

CZ 7-10 HZ 1-10

 ↕ 25cm ↔ 40cm Nov-Feb

Sedum MATRONA

Sedum

- AUTUMN JOY *S. spectabile* — Many think this is the finest perennial, being such a chameleon. Starting with grey toothed succulent leaves in spring that produce broccoli-like green heads, changing from deep pink to bronze-copper, and heads of black seeds in winter. Combines beautifully with grasses. ↕ 70cm ↔ 50cm
- MATRONA — Maroon stems and flat top flower heads of white buds. Pale-pink flower heads fade to reddish-brown. ↕ 70cm ↔ 50cm

CZ 7-11 HZ 1-9   Dec-Apr

Verbena bonariensis

Loved by butterflies and bees, this easiest of plants to grow flowering continuously, standing tall with lilac purple clusters 5cm across. A see-through self supporting flower at home with pastel, plum or silver colour schemes.

CZ 9-10 HZ 1-10

 ↕ 2m ↔ 45cm Dec-Apr

Goldenrod

Solidago 'Golden Baby' — Late summer sprays of yellow lighten the lazy autumn afternoons. Good cut flower and companion to asters and particularly *Anemone scabiosa*.

CZ 7-11 HZ 1-7

    ↕ 80cm ↔ 80cm Oct-Mar

Lamb's Ears

Shrubs

Some of the most popular shrubs have serious garden deficiencies.

Azaleas and rhododendrons are often brash in spring and are dull throughout summer. Camellia foliage is too gloomy in winter and drab in summer. Crepe myrtles have good bark but the summer flowers are too bright for our intense heat. It is worth considering using fruiting shrubs like pomegranates, persimmons, custard apples and avocados, as they have fine form and work well as garden shrubs.

Evergreen EXCEPTIONALLY FRAGRANT

Angels Trumpet

Brugmansia — This fragrant shrub has a place in every frost free garden. Pendulous trumpets hang from drought tolerant foliage and have three spectacular flowerings, filling the garden with perfume. New colours in red, yellow, peach and white single or double blooms. Handle carefully.

CZ 10-12 HZ 3-10

 5m ↔ 3m Oct-Mar

Cherry Pie

Heliotropium arborescens — Vanilla scented flowers fill the Heronswood garden for 9 months of the year. The original species has the strongest scent with pale and dark violet flowers.

* LORD ROBERTS — Tightly packed, deep violet flowers sit neatly above the outstanding dark foliage.
* GOLDEN — With lime green foliage and tiny white flowers, this is the perfect plant to lighten up a shady spot.

CZ 10-11 HZ 1-11

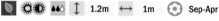 1.2m ↔ 1m Sep-Apr

Buddleja Butterfly Bush

* B. salvifolia — Honey scented, lilac blooms are an autumn bonus for this evergreen shrub or windbreak for angry climates. ☉ Mar-May
* B. davidii 'Lochinch' — The choice summer flowering blue butterfly bush because its silver foliage highlights pale blue flowers. ☉ Nov-Feb

CZ 8-11 HZ 1-11 3m ↔ 2m

Night Scented Jessamine

Cestrum nocturnun — Most *cestrums* flower through the day but this one's lime-green insignificant flowers open in the evening, sending its perfume into every corner of the garden. Tough and drought tolerant it's a "plant and forget" shrub until the hot summer nights.

CZ 10-12 HZ 3-10

3m ↔ 1.5m Oct-Mar

Orange Jessamine

Murraya paniculata — The ultimate shrub for a summer garden with the cooling effect of white flowers. Creamy-white, orange blossom-scented flowers that last all summer fit elegantly against the dark foliage. Glossy aromatic green foliage is easily hedged. Fast growing in humid summers.

CZ 10-12 HZ 4-11

 3m ↔ 2m Dec-Mar

Tree Gardenia

Gardenia thunbergia — The ultimate plants are worth waiting for. Imagine sitting under the umbrella of hundreds of gardenia flowers that uncoil like a pinwheel into intensely fragrant single white flowers. Cool glossy, foliage. We planted four shrubs 25 years ago at Heronswood.

CZ 9b-12 HZ 4-11

 3m ↔ 3m Jan-Mar

Deciduous

Lilac

Syringa vulgaris — If it weren't for its beautiful perfume this shrub would hardly be noticed. Plant breeders have over worked this shrub into larger double flowers for the vase, but we prefer the simplicity of original garden blooms. White, lilac, lilac-red, single or double flowers.

CZ 7-10 HZ 1-6

3m ↔ 2m Oct

Cherry Pie GOLDEN

Angels Trumpet

Lilac

Cherry Pie PURPLE

Tree Gardenia

Butterfly Bush

Orange Jessamine

Buddleja salvifolia

Magnolia PINK

Hydrangea OAK LEAF

Hydrangea

Flowering Quince

Smoke Bush GRACE

Viburnum opulus

Black Elder GUINCHO PURPLE

Hydrangea

From the cool woodlands of Asia and North America, hydrangeas are restricted to shady, cool and moist areas of the garden in the Mediterranean climates with long, hot summers. Enjoy the flowers on hot afternoons from a shady hammock.

- GARDEN *H. macrophylla* — Gigantic mop-head flowers in pewter blue in 5.5pH or less or pink in alkaline 5.5pH plus. 2m tall bushes have dull green leaves that need the flowers because the bush is dull. Excellent dried flowers. ↕ 2m ↔ 2.5m
- OAKLEAF *H. quercifoclia* — Deciduous white conical flowers and deep red autumn foliage. ↕ 2m ↔ 2.5m
- *H. paniculata grandiflora* — Tree-like, large 30cm creamy flowers on a vigorous deciduous shrub. Best grown in shady shrub borders. ↕ 3.7m ↔ 2.5m

CZ 8-11 HZ 1-6  Jan-Mar

Flowering Quince

Chaenomeles japonica — We treasure the 40 year old hedge that encloses our St Erth garden with thorny stems to deter kangaroos and abundant red, pink or white spring flowers followed by edible fruit.

CZ 8-10 HZ 1-7  Jul-Aug

Magnolia

Magnolia x soulangeana — Is it the first shrub to flower? Exquisitely shaped goblets are followed by beautiful, light green leaves and handsome form. Needs moist, fertile soil.

CZ 7-11 HZ 1-7 6m ↔ 5m Aug-Sep

Viburnum

Rather flat deciduous foliage and form is tolerated because shrubs are tough.

- *V. x burkwoodii* — Intensely fragrant.
- *V. opulus* — Sterile. Huge snowball flowers.

CZ 7-10 HZ 1-6  2m ↔ 2m Aug-Oct

Smoke Bush

Cotinus coggygria — The smoke bush goes through three transformations. Starting with green or bronze round leaves in spring, then producing plume-like panicles of flower in summer and finishing with a vibrant autumnal display. Drought tolerant.

- YOUNG LADY — Compact leaves suit small gardens. ↕ 2m ↔ 2m
- GRACE — Oval purple leaves, purple pink smoked panicles. ↕ 3m ↔ 2m

CZ 7-10 HZ 1-8 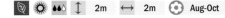 3m ↔ 2m Nov-Dec

Black Elder

Sambacus nigra 'Guincho Purple'— This is the common elder with prodigious yielding elderberry flowers and berries to turn into wine. Purple foliage is a useful contrast compared with the dominant greens found in most gardens. A fast growing useful shrub.

CZ 7-11 HZ 1-10  6m ↔ 6m Nov-Jan

Evergreen shrubs

Honey Bush

Melianthus major — This outstanding foliage plant seems more like a fleshy perennial than a shrub. Heavily toothed, glaucous leaves enjoy the heat and drought. We prune off the brick red flower spikes and renew new foliage by cutting to ground level in late winter.

CZ 7-11 HZ 1-7

🌿 ☀ ◌◌◌ ↕ 2m ↔ 2m ⊙ Sep-Nov

Ceonothus Yankee Point

Ceonothus griseus horizontalis — The very commonly planted Blue Pacific is so vibrant a colour that it destroys the peace and harmony of the garden. *It would be better if it never flowered but then its foliage is really boring!* This horizontal form with its shiny green leaves and pale-blue flowers, however, fits elegantly in the landscape.

CZ 9a-11 HZ 1-6

🌿 ☀ ◌◌◌ ↕ 90cm ↔ 3m ⊙ Oct-Nov

Myrtus tarentina

As tightly knit as box but faster growing with white fluffy myrtle flowers and aromatic foliage. Tight packed leaves respond to clipping and dry heat.

CZ 9a-11 HZ 1-11

🌿 ☀ ◌◌◌ ↕ 1m ↔ 1m ⊙ Nov-Dec

Box

Buxus sempervirens — Its dense glossy tightly packed leaves make sharp edges perfect for the lush green formal hedging or into mounds and topiary.

CZ 7-10 HZ 1-7

🌿 ☀☀ ◌◌◌ ↕ 60cm ↔ 30cm

Bridal Veil

Retama monosperma — The best non-invasive broom providing a curtain of fragrant white flowers and elegant weeping branches when flowering is finished. Just the tone and texture for seaside gardens with its weeping form.

CZ 9a-11 HZ 1-8

🌿 ☀ ◌◌◌ ↕ 3m ↔ 1.5m ⊙ Sep-Oct

Wigandia

Wigandia caracasana — As spectacular in flower as echium Heronswood Blue with identical flower colour. It has the bonus of bold leaves, an essential background to any evergreen garden. Combine with honey bush and *romneya* to create a cool appeal in the toughest summer.

CZ 9b-11 HZ 1-10

🌿 ☀ ◌◌◌ ↕ 2m ↔ 3m ⊙ Sep-Nov

Box

Ceonothus YANKEE POINT

Tree Lupin

Lupinus arboreus — Rapid growing, first year flowering shrub that hold spikes of white or golden yellow candles. Grey-green, lupin-like leaves. Nitrogen fixing.

CZ 9-11 HZ 1-7

🌿 ☀ ◌◌◌ ↕ 1.5m ↔ 1.5m ⊙ Oct-Dec

Phlomis Lemon Blush

P. purpurea x crinata — Whorls of primrose lemon flowers are more easily integrated than other phlomis. Soft felted grey foliage enhances the flower platforms.

CZ 9a-10 HZ 1-10

🌿 ☀ ◌◌◌ ↕ 1.2m ↔ 1m ⊙ Oct-Dec

Echium Pride of Madeira

E. candicans — Thriving in 40°C heat and 200mm rainfall this fast growing grey foliage shrub produces masses of vertical candles in spring as striking as any lupin. Cut off spent flower spikes to renew good plant habit.

SHRUBBY ECHIUMS

* HERONSWOOD BLUE — Cool, sky-blue selection from our garden.

* HERONSWOOD PINK — Mid pink candles.

BIENNIAL ECHIUMS (die after flowering)

* *E. simplex* — Single white column to 1.5m.

* *E. wildpretii* — Spectacular, rusty-red, fat spikes to 1 metre.

* *E. pininana* — Columns reaching to 5m flower at Heronswood in white, purple or blue before dying.

CZ 9b-11 HZ 4-12

🌿 ☀☀ ◌◌◌ ↕ 2m ↔ 2m ⊙ Sep-Nov

Wigandia

Echium HERONSWOOD PINK & BLUE

Bridal Veil

Myrtus tarentina

Phlomis LEMON BLUSH

Honey Bush

Fruiting shrubs

Blueberry

Chilean Guava

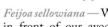

Guava PINEAPPLE

Natal Plum

True Curry Leaf

Natal Plum

Carissa grandiflora — I germinated seeds 35 years ago and this elegant evergreen shrub is now extensively planted at Heronswood. Very fragrant white flowers on thick dark leaves with spines provide red plum size berries. Needs heat but very drought tolerant.

CZ 10-11 HZ 3-9

🍃 ☀️🌤️ 💧💧 ↕️ 2.5m ↔️ 2m ○ Mar-Apr

Guava Strawberry

Psidium littorale var. longipes — The cinnamon mottling of its bark, the dark red (or yellow) berries and puffs of flowers are all appealing attractions of this useful garden shrub. As handsome as any crepe myrtle, why not enjoy edible fruit as well?

CZ 9b-11 HZ 1-7

🍃 ☀️🌤️ 💧💧 ↕️ 4m ↔️ 3m ○ Feb-Apr

Guava Pineapple

Feijoa sellowiana — We have a hedge of feijoas in front of our avocados because the felty, green foliage looks handsome, but it can be grown as a small tree. Bright callistemon-red flowers produce torpedo shaped exceptionally green fruit with a delectable aroma.

CZ 9-11 HZ 1-8

🍃 ☀️ 💧💧💧 ↕️ 4m ↔️ 3m ○ Apr-Jul

Blueberry

Vaccinium sp. — Imagine how much improved your garden would be if you replaced all the azaleas and rhododendrons with blueberries, because they too like shade, water, and acid soils. Flowers are pink and lantern-like, berries blue and foliage turns red-orange.

- HIGH BUSH — 🍂 Deciduous forms for high chill frosty areas.
- LOW BUSH — 🍃 Evergreen Sunshine Blue.

CZ 7-10 HZ 1-6

☀️ 💧💧💧 ↕️ 2.5m ↔️ 1.5m ○ Dec-Feb

Chilean Guava

Ugni molinae — Also known as Tassie Berry, this makes a great hedge and its small, eucalyptus-like flowers produces delectable berries. Thrives in hot conditions and is a tougher alternative to box.

CZ 8-10 HZ 2-7

🍃 ☀️ 💧💧💧 ↕️ 1.5m ↔️ 1.3m ○ Feb-Apr

True Curry Leaf

Murraya koenigii — Our tree at Heronswood is thriving, so this shouldn't be confined to the tropics. Umbrella-shaped habit with handsome, lush green foliage which, when picked, produces a madras-like curry flavour.

CZ 10-11 HZ 1-12

🍃 ☀️🌤️ 💧💧💧 ↕️ 3m ↔️ 2m

Lemon Verbena

Pomegranate

Punica granatum — Most gardeners know only of orange flowered pomegranates but pink and white flower forms exist. But the magic is when large showy fruit hang from glistening green foliage in autumn.

* ELCITE — Large yellow skinned fruit expose delicious red seeds that hang on the bush.
* ANDRE LE ROI — Salmon coloured double flowers with tiny fruit.
* DOUBLE WHITE

CZ 9b-11 HZ 4-12

🍃 ☀ ᗊᗊᗊ ↕ 4m ↔ 2m ◯ Feb-Apr

Bay

Laurus nobilis — The Bay leaf used in cooking survives extreme heat and dry soil. As a tree it is used in Italy as a taller version of the box hedge, trimmed as a focal topiary or a simple evergreen in a shrubbery.

CZ 7-10 HZ 3-10

🍃 ☀☀ ᗊᗊᗊ ↕ 10m ↔ 7m

Lemon Verbena

Aloysia citriodora — Outstanding hedge for fresh picked leaf tea. Survived the scorching 800 degree heat of our restaurant fire. Intensely fragrant fresh or dried leaves are bright green scenting the air with lemon.

CZ 10-12 HZ 3-8

🍃 ☀ ᗊᗊᗊ ↕ 1.5m ↔ 1m ◉ Oct-Mar

Tea Camellia

Camellia sinensis — Instead of growing common camellias, try the one that is everyone's favourite beverage. A slow growing evergreen that thrives in humidity. Glossy leaves, small white or pink single flowers with yellow stamens. Clip to a tight hedge for picking, as they do at Cloudehill. ↕ 1m ↔ 1m

* FISHTAIL *C. japonica* — Fishtail leaf form, as if it has done the splits! Double pink with yellow stamens. ↕ 4m ↔ 2m

CZ 9b-11 HZ 1-7 🍃 ☀☀ ᗊᗊᗊ ◉ Apr-Jun

Pomegranate ANDRE LE ROI

Loquat

Eriobotrya japonica — Dense, dark leathery leaves provide cool shade and heavy crops of yellow fruit. Drought tolerant.

* NAGASAKIWASE — Self-pollinating.

CZ 9b-11 HZ 3-8

🍃 ☀ ᗊᗊᗊ ↕ 7m ↔ 5m ◯ Sep-Oct

Juniper Berry

Juniperus communis — Also known as Gin Berry, it has elegant evergreen foliage that works so well in our border. Self-fertile, yielding berries for gin.

CZ 7-10 HZ 1-7

🍃 ☀☀ ᗊᗊᗊ ↕ 4m ↔ 1.5m ◯ Aug-Nov

Quince

Cydonia oblonga — The quince in flower is the equal of an old shrub rose with single pinkish-white, open blooms. The large yellow fruit are aromatic and a true delight of autumn when cooked. Enjoys heat and drought and provides golden autumn leaves. ↕ 2.5m ↔ 5m

* CHINESE QUINCE *C. sinensis* — Makes a dense packed hedge with gigantic yellow fruit and textured bark. ↕ 5m ↔ 5m

CZ 8-10 HZ 1-8

🍃 ☀☀ ᗊᗊᗊ ↕ 5m ↔ 5m ◯ Mar-Apr

Juniper Berry

Quince

Loquat

Tea

Pomegranate ELCITE

Bay

Avocado

Babaco

Golden Fruit of the Andes

White Sapote

Custard Apple

Coffee

Japanese Pepper

Coffee

Coffea arabica — Growing in the shade of tropical rainforests, this handsome shrub has fragrant white flowers to offset glossy dark evergreen leaves before the red fruits appear to hold the beans. Protect from sun and frost as we have at Heronswood.

CZ 10-11 HZ 4-12

🌼 ⚫⚫⚫ ↕ 2m ↔ 1m ◯ Oct-Jun

White Sapote

Casimiroa edulis — Once tasted everyone wants to grow it, but because it ripens so quickly it is never offered in the shops. But it is a first rate shade tree with vigorous rainforest like five fingered leaves and custard, creamy soft fleshy fruit. Prune out central leader to create bush habit. Maybell's Variety is self-pollinating.

CZ 10-12 HZ 4-12

🌼🌼 ⚫⚫◇ ↕ 10m ↔ 6m ◯ Mar-May

Golden Fruit of the Andes

Solanum quitoense — 'Naranjilla' is the name Spanish speakers give this beautiful foliage plant of huge, flat furry leaves with purple veins that hide white flowers and orange fruit, the juice of which is said to be the finest in the world.

CZ 10-12 HZ 4-14

🌼🌼 ⚫⚫◇ ↕ 2m ↔ 2m ◯ Feb-Apr

Avocado

Persea americana — Why not plant an edible dense leafed avocado instead of a camellia? They grow in identical conditions in all coastal capital cities but reward with 200-300 delicious fruit each year. By pruning to a picking height of 2m only and keeping in perfectly drained soil they are an excellent screen.

- HASS — Fruit will store well and turn green to black when ripe. Type A that is self-pollinating for cooler winter flowering.
- BACON — For north and south, warm and cool springs, type B that assists Hass.

CZ 9b-11 HZ 4-9

🌼🌼 ⚫⚫⚫ ↕ 10m ↔ 6m ◯ All year

Babaco/Champagne Fruit

Carica pentagonia — No tree captures the tropical look more completely than babaco. This cold tolerant form is fast growing, producing elongated yellow hanging fruit, tasting sweet and zesty.

CZ 10-12 HZ 3-11

🌼 ⚫⚫◇ ↕ 2.5m ↔ 1.5m ◯ Nov-Mar

Japanese Pepper

Zanthoxylum piperitum — Sichuan pepper is a first rate foliage plant that thrives from Tasmania to the tropics with emerald green, aromatic deciduous leaves and pepper-like berries.

CZ 9a-11 HZ 4-7

🌼🌼 ⚫⚫◇ ↕ 2m ↔ 1.5m ◯ Oct-Dec

Custard Apple Cherimoya

Anona cherimola — This is a beautiful, small foliage tree with grey bark, good form and it provides dessert fruit at Heronswood. The visual equal of a persimmon.

CZ 10-11 HZ 4-9

🌼 ⚫⚫◇ ↕ 6m ↔ 6m ◯ Feb-Jun

Climbers – edibles and ornamental

Snail Creeper

Solanum wendlandii

Grape

Vitis vinifera — For thousands of years Greeks and Romans have sheltered from the hot sun and picked their grapes as the tastiest fruit dessert. Just provide a pergola near the house, and its leaf fall will let in precious winter sun.

- BLACK MUSCAT — The sweetest purple dessert that rarely appears because it won't last 30 days like supermarket driven grapes. The oldest domesticated wine sources for raisins, liqueur, muscat, muscato and orange muscat.

- *V. labrusca* 'Concord' — Musky aromatic flavoured purple grape that is used for the table juice and wine. Leaves have grey underside.

CZ 9b-12 HZ 2-8

    ☀ ▲▲◊ ↕ 4m ↔ 4m ◯ Dec-Jan

Solanum wendlandii

One of the world's most spectacular climbers and a feature at Heronswood. The Costa Rican nightshade has 50 cent-size lavender flowers that keep coming for months. Fleshy leaves drop in coolish winters but evergreen in the tropics. Needs heat from a north facing wall and wire as support for the climb.

CZ 10-13 HZ 4-11

☀ ▲▲◊ ↕ 5m ↔ 5m ◉ Dec-Apr

Snail Creeper

Vigna caracalla — Intensely fragrant flowers have intriguing spirals of snail shell-like white and purple flowers. Deciduous bean-like foliage.

CZ 9b-11 HZ 2-12

  ☀ ▲▲◊ ↕ 6m ↔ 2m ◉ Jan-Mar

Chilean Jasmine

Mandevilla laxa — This mandevilla is the most fragrant of the summer climbers and will climb through shrubs to shine with its white trumpets of flowers.

CZ 7-10 HZ 1-7

 ☀☀ ▲▲◊ ↕ 3m ↔ 6m ◉ Dec-Feb

Passionfruit

Passiflora edulis — Hide a fence or screen a garden shed with this rapid growing vine of exquisite crucifix-like flowers with purple, juicy fruits. Protect from wind and keep moist through summer.

CZ 9b-10 HZ 3-11

 ☀☀ ▲▲◊ ↕ 3m ↔ 6m ◯ Sep-May

Kiwifruit

Actinidia chinensis 'Hayward' — This rampant vine needs similar support to wisteria, the hairy green-fleshed fruit hang from metre long arching branches that need support 1.5m above the ground. Needs male and female flowering vines, wind protection and fertile, moist soil.

- *A. arguta* 'Issai' — Date sized hairless green fruit are self-pollinating and eaten skin and all.

CZ 7-11 HZ 4-8

 ☀ ▲▲◊ ↕ 7m ↔ 5m ◯ May-Jul

Chilean Jasmine

Kiwifruit

Passionfruit

Grape MUSCAT

Kiwiberry ARGUTA

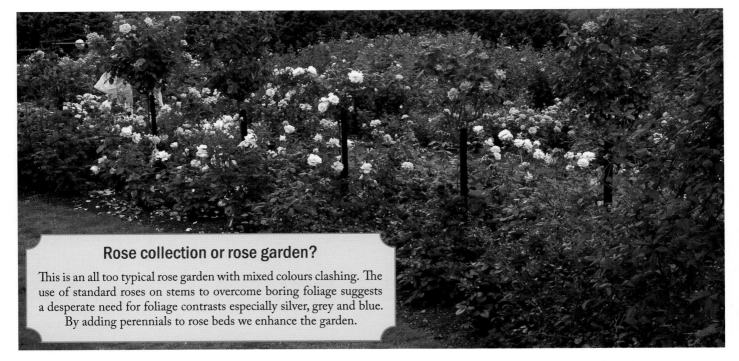

Rose collection or rose garden?

This is an all too typical rose garden with mixed colours clashing. The use of standard roses on stems to overcome boring foliage suggests a desperate need for foliage contrasts especially silver, grey and blue. By adding perennials to rose beds we enhance the garden.

Multiflora Single Rose

Think of roses as shrubs with exuberant growth, despite having no scent or picking possibilities.

Russian Sage

Airy flowering perennials, particularly of blue, naturally link to yellow, pink or white roses.

Rosa sericea

Rosa sericea species rose has interesting stems, foliage and hips to extend interest.

Carpet Rose

Carpet roses have been bred for freeways and for landscapes, not gardens.

Iceberg Bush

Typical floribunda rose. Lots of flowers that integrate too rigidly with perennials and shrubs.

Hybrid Tea Rose

This rose was never bred for garden display, just for the vase.

Roses for the garden

With thousands of rose cultivars to choose from, how could a selection be reduced?

Roses are undoubtedly the world's most popular and attractive flower, attracting enthusiasts for over 2000 years, but do they have a place in the gardens of the discerning?

Just as sugar has entered our diet and become the single most popular food, creating obesity and threatening a century of progress towards a long and healthy life, the ubiquity of the rose is destroying the quality of our gardens not just in Australia, but throughout the world. There may not be any plant for some gardeners that has the fragrance, beauty or bud form of a rose but that doesn't make a rose garden-worthy.

The roses we have selected are chosen for their form in helping create beautiful garden pictures. We've omitted hybrid tea bushes as they are ugly, spiky in form and are best for picking and enjoying in a vase. We've avoided floribundas too, as they are a colour overload devoid of form like annual bedding plants.

Pat Austin

DAVID AUSTIN SHRUB ROSES

A 60 year rose breeding project to combine the shape and scent of old roses with repeat flowering has transformed our gardens.

Created for beauty in the garden not the vase, they have short stems and "multiflora flowering habit", creating better garden specimens and improving the number of plants that enhance a summer garden. They thrive and grow more vigorously in hot dry climates.

CZ 7-10 HZ 1-13   Name / year of introduction

🍃 ☀ 💧 ✤ 𝑓 ✂ ◉ Nov-Apr

Golden Celebration 1992

Golden apricot cupped flowers with mid green leaves and long arching stems. Can be trained up a pillar. Yellow blooms warm a spring garden like a beacon on a green lawn. ↕ 1.2m ↔ 1m

Cymbeline 1982

Vigorous healthy dark green leaves provide the background for cupped grey pink buds that can be a pillar or pegged down to become a hedge. ↕ 2m ↔ 1.5m

Mary Rose 1988

The most popular David Austin because its quilled pale pink blooms fade a paler blush. The most desired colour in roses, it's cupped, fragrant and is early and long blooming. ↕ 1.5m ↔ 1.5m

Graham Thomas

Heritage

Pat Austin 1995

Fancy carrying the Austin name and not being a pastel pink! Copper blooms are cupped and fade to yellow and cream and it makes a wonderful hedge. ↕ 1.2m ↔ 1.2m

Graham Thomas 1983

The best yellow Austin celebrates great 20th century gardener Graham Thomas. Cupped golden yellow blooms fade to yellow. The plant can reach 4-5m in our climate. Strong fragrance. ↕ 3m ↔ 3m

Gertrude Jekyll 1986

This immensely vigorous shrub carries the name of another of England's pioneers of 20th century gardening, who authored the classic *The Making Of A Garden*. Rich dark pink cupped blooms are very fragrant and fade to pale pink. ↕ 2m ↔ 1.5m

Gertrude Jekyll

Golden Celebration

Cymbeline

Mary Rose

Heritage shrub roses

Buffy Beauty

Pierre de Ronsard

Souvenir de la Malmaison

Rosa rugosa species

Mutabalis

Canary Bird

Mme Isaac Pereire

In avoiding hybrid teas and floribundas, which are really like candy floss on a stick, we have listed elegant heritage shrubs and the best of the David Austin repeat flowering roses that can enhance your garden with foliage and form.

CZ 7-10 HZ 1-13   Name / type / year of introduction

Buff Beauty HYBRID MUSK 1939

Double flowers of apricot and soft orange in a rich buff. Fragrant and repeat throughout summer and autumn and sometimes in early winter. Can be trained as a climber too.

↕ 2m ↔ 1.5m ⊙ Nov-May

Canary Bird 1907

With dainty light green leaflets and purplish black hips, its foliage is handsome and disease free. Single flowered canary yellow blooms appear along prickly stems.

↕ 2.4m ↔ 4m ⊙ Nov-Dec

Rosa rugosa species

Vigorous enough to plant in a sand dune or freeway median strip, it meets all criteria for garden-worthiness. Continuous single white or magenta-pink blooms provide large red hips from healthy bright green rugose leaflets that turn yellow. This wild rose ticks all the boxes modern bred hybrid teas and floribundas roses don't.

↕ 1.2m ↔ 1.4m ⊙ Nov-Apr

Ispahan DAMASK c1832

Rose expert author Charles Quest-Ritson says *"If you have room for no more than one old rose ... Isphanan is the best of the once flowering old garden roses"*. First to flower, evergreen, clusters of delicious scented large mid pink blooms.

↕ 2m ↔ 2m ⊙ Oct-Jan

Mme Isaac Pereire BOURBON 1881

Opulent blooms with sumptuous scent that will cause swooning! Dark cerise flowers faded to silver pink from late spring to autumn which combines with blue and purple. Can be grown as shrub or pillar rose.

↕ 2.5m ↔ 2m ⊙ Nov-Apr

Mutabalis CHINA ROSE 1900

Continuous flowering genes come from China roses and this one is never out of bloom making it a very precious shrub. Beginning buff yellow it turns pink and finally crimson.

↕ 2m ↔ 2.5m ⊙ Nov-Apr

Pierre de Ronsard MODERN SHRUB 1987

A very modern bred rose like David Austin's that has the attraction of heavy flowers that hang down but are cupped and full. Ivory coloured buds deepening to light pink at the centre. Pillar or shrub.

↕ 3m ↔ 2m ⊙ Nov-Apr

Souvenir de la Malmaison BOURBON 1843

"Quilled and quartered" is the concept David Austin followed in his modern breeding. Beginning soft fresh pink with magnificent scent and continuous flowering it has just one catch. It doesn't like cold and wet but thrives in hot dry climates.

↕ 3m ↔ 2m ⊙ Nov-Apr

Zephirine Drouhin

Black Boy

Crépuscule

Lorraine Lee

Nancy Hayward

Mermaid

ALISTER CLARK'S AUSTRALIAN BRED CLIMBERS

40 years of breeding for the hot Australian sun yielded 130 new cultivars, and these three are some of his most successful roses.

Black Boy 1919

Is this the closest to black a crimson rose gets? Raised in 1919 by Australia's own Alister Clark, Black Boy is still the most popular crimson climber. Outer petals are a deeper shade than within, and they darken with age to develop subtle purple black markings. The first flowers are early, appearing mid-spring, followed by a second flush during summer. A vigorous climber for pillars, fences and arbours, Black Boy will infuse your garden with its fresh apple scent.

↕ 2.5m ↔ 2m ⊛ Nov-Apr

Lorraine Lee 1924

Blooms throughout the year. Exceptional in that it does so in winter and early spring when every other rose is waking up. Double pink fragrant blooms on evergreen foliage.

↕ 3m ↔ 2.5m ⊛ All year

Nancy Hayward 1937

Bred from *Rosa gigantea* to cope with intensely hot summers, its huge single vivid pink blooms are striking, even during winter and spring.

↕ 6m ↔ 4m ⊛ All year

Crépuscule NOISETTE 1904

Almost always in flower and one of the most beautiful roses of all. Flowers open rich copper and fade to buff with strong delicious scent. Its thornless stem suits budding to tall standard roses or a slow growing climber.

↕ 5m ↔ 5m ⊛ Nov-Mar

Zephirine Drouhin BOURBON 1818

A continuously flowering thornless rose that is first and last to flower. Bury your nose in its petals to enjoy a delicious delirium; ideal as a pillar or climber.

↕ 3m ↔ 2m ⊛ Nov-Apr

Rosa x centifolia 1596

With over 100 petals hence the name of this famous cabbage rose with its huge blooms that make a goblet of rose pink. Excellent fragrance.

↕ 1.5m ↔ 1.5m ⊛ Nov-Dec

Mermaid 1918

This *bracteata* hybrid features soft-yellow single petals with deep gold stamens and it flowers continuously. Foliage is bright and evergreen in all but cold climates. Whilst slow to establish, it will ascend garages, sheds or walls without pruning.

↕ 5m ↔ 4m ⊛ Nov-Apr

Rosa x centifolia

Heritage climbers

Albertine

Rambling Rector

Veilchenblau

Masquerade

Multiflora Species

On arches, arbours, fences and sheds, these climbers are foundation plants that give great beauty to garden structures.

CZ 7-10 HZ 1-13   Name / type / year of introduction

Albertine 1921

Few roses have the scent and bud charm of salmon pink blooms, opening from darker buds. Vigorous and prickly, it ascends walls or clambers through trees, but can also be grown as a 2m free standing shrub. Incredible 8 week display.

↕ 3.5m ↔ 1.5m ◉ Dec-Feb

Rosa laevigata species

A friend celebrated his 90th birthday surrounded by literally thousands of blooms of this exquisite single rose with golden stamens. Shiny green leaves that last all year, with bright orange hips in autumn.

↕ 5m ↔ 5m ◉ Nov-Jan

Veilchenblau MULTIFLORA 1909

The most popular purple rambler that is striking amongst almost all other colours. Flower colour holds on the plant as it fades, losing red tints and finishing lilac grey. Pale green foliage with orange hips from vigorous double blooms.

↕ 3m ↔ 2m ◉ Nov-Dec

Masquerade FLORIBUNDA 1958

This oddity deserves a place because of its floral gymnastics. Flowers open bright yellow fading to pink and then deep crimson. Clusters of 10-20 semi-double flowers produce red hips and repeat continuously. The show is bizarre, conspicuous and quite fascinating.

↕ 4m ↔ 2m ◉ Nov-Apr

Multiflora species

Visiting Ted Treloar, the acclaimed rose grower, after walking through all the new varieties, this was what excited me most. It will grow into a billowing impenetrable hedge that's exquisitely beautiful – a better animal barrier than fence posts and much cheaper too. Its entry into the nursery trade is via the name Cottage Garden Rose, and it is the most used root stock for budding on it is so vigorous. Pink or white.

↕ 3m ↔ 3m ◉ Nov-Dec

Rambling Rector MULTIFLORA 1900

Presumably found in an Irish rectory garden, it has the vigour of multiflora but airy clusters of small double creamy white flowers followed by orange hips. Foliage is pale green and it is a stunning sight at Roseraie de L'Hay gardens in Paris. Can be trained to a 2 metre shrub.

↕ 3.5m ↔ 2m ◉ Nov-Dec

Where have all the hips gone?

The concealment of flower stamens by continuously breeding tightly packed rose buds for the vase means today's modern roses do not pollinate and produce beautiful hips enclosing seeds.

Perennial companions for a rose garden

Golden Celebration Rose

French Lavender

Mme Isaac Pereire

Wormwood

Catmint

Lamb's Ears

Perennials for a rose garden

The most popular flower, the rose, is now so over planted that we gardeners at Diggers have largely avoided including roses in our plantings until this year.

It is of course easier to criticise a plant with defects than is it to create a rose garden that is beautiful. For us it created a sort of visual indigestion; clearly a diet of roses alone, to use a food analogy, is rather like eating a 400 gram steak without vegetables.

So our solution, when creating a rose garden at St Erth, was not to concentrate on exclusive rose plantings but to create our own version of a rose garden by enhancing our plantings with silver textured companionable shrubs and perennials to create a contrast of foliage and to add a softening texture to the drab green foliage of the typical rose.

Our second lesson from visiting rose gardens is that they must have physical structures because their straggly form needs the support of steel arches to clamber over and through. This structure also creates another dimension to this natural woodland scene with its formal pathway that leads the visitor to a shady rose bower to rest and view the rest of the garden.

Colour schemes

We chose to limit our rose selection colours to yellow and white with splashes of blue from well chosen perennials.

This colour range is harmonious with the colours of St Erth's spring daffodils but also helps to merge in with the green lawn to draw the visitors eyes up into the garden.

We have kept our dominating pink and red coloured roses to fit in with colour schemes in other parts of the garden (there is a place for every colour in a garden but never in the same visual frame).

So in our rose garden we have avoided selecting the modern hybrid teas and floribundas and concentrated on old fashioned ramblers and climbers and shrubs that are chosen for their ability to repeat flower.

Our choice of grey foliage

There are lots of greys to choose but we have consciously planted the beds with more grey plants than roses so it could just as easily be called a silver garden. To provide height that covers the mid foreground in front of the drab foliage of shrub roses, the obvious choice is catmint because it flowers so long and it is available in different heights and there is even a white form.

Artemisia Powis Castle, catmint, santolina, any lavender (but particularly English lavender which flowers in January) and the autumn flowering Mexican sage.

125

Trees – are eucalypts garden-worthy?

Eucalypts dominate the Australian continent like no other tree anywhere else in the world.

Eucalypt leaves hang vertically from their branches so the sun passes straight through, with little shade protection for the soil and plants beneath.

This characteristic, combined with their massive litter drop of dry leaves and bark, creates a landscape so flammable that fires destroy towns, animals and gardens. So planting eucalypts in a garden can potentially create an atmosphere that puts a gardener's lifetime of work at risk.

Who would have thought that a bushfire would threaten suburban Dromana so close to CFA access with a freeway 200m away?

The bushfire that destroyed our thatch roof restaurant and offices at Heronswood not only destroyed a building, but a special place that was close to the hearts of all of us that worked there for 18 years. These fires destroy our understories of native perennials and shrubs that fill ecological niches in every ecosystem.

After a fire eucalypts quickly recover, either from underground ligno-tubers or epicormic buds in the tree trunks, so fire helps them dominate the landscape.

Australia is probably hotter, drier and with the world's most exhausted soils as a consequence. The 'eucalyptic' is a more serious predator than the shark, snake or crocodile and it can't even move. As gardeners we need to make tree planting choices to protect our houses from inflammable 'eucalyptic'.

As an alternative, we should look to Australian rainforest and edible trees.

Tree selector
Rainforest evergreens

🌳 Growth rates: Slow = 30cm/year   Fast = 1m/year

Black Booyong

Argyrodendron actinophyllum — This rapid growing rainforest tree from NSW is exceptionally drought tolerant, grows in full sun and produces large buttresses that are very eye catching. Its glossy, seven fingered leaves create a cooling effect. Thrives in Melbourne's Botanic Gardens and at Heronswood.

CZ 9b-10 **HZ** 4-8 🌳 Fast
🍃 ☀☀ ▲◇◇ ↕ 15m ↔ 8m

Flame Tree

Brachychiton acerifolius — Our most popular rainforest tree due to its spectacular display in spring and summer, when the Flame Tree drops all its leaves, bursting into flower followed by curious mice-like pods, in which it forms its seeds. Maple-like evergreen shiny leaves and in flower it is as breath taking as a Canadian autumn.

CZ 9b-13 **HZ** 4-8 🌳 Medium
🍃 ☀☀ ▲◇◇ ↕ 15m ↔ 8m ⚙ Nov-Feb

Native Frangipani

Hymenosporum flavum — The exceptional perfume comes from the native frangipani's striking yellow spring flowers which is reason enough to grow one. Shiny, dark green pittosporum-like foliage is easily seen through so a regular prune will restrain its height and keep a shape neat.

CZ 9b-13 **HZ** 4-8 🌳 Medium
🍃 ☀☀ ▲◇◇ ↕ 12m ↔ 6m ⚙ Sep-Oct

Flame Tree

Black Booyong

Native Frangipani

Flindersia australis

Australian Red Cedar

Toona ciliata — Red cedars are one of the finest trees in the Adelaide Botanic Garden and deserve planting throughout Australia. Their growth is rapid, stature handsome and leaves long and graceful. Over-logged for timber that was used to build furniture, it needs a revival. A number one choice for large gardens.

CZ 9b-13 HZ 4-8   Fast
15-20m ↔ 8-10m

Lilly Pilly

Syzygium smithii — In colder southern zones this provides the ultimate replacement for eucalypts. It provides cool shade (10°C cooler at 40°C than under a eucalypt), refreshing foliage at a moderate height and it's not a fire risk. Found in rainforests from Wilsons Promontory to Queensland, the Lilly Pilly provides pinkish-purple berries in winter, fluffy white summer flowers and dense dark green shiny leaves that can be hedged or left to form a statuesque tree. Rarely affected by psyllids.

CZ 9a-10 HZ 1-7   Fast
12m ↔ 6m   Mar-May

Macadamia

Macadamia tetraphylla — Our Australian contribution to the international food scene. Ornamental tassels of pink flowers transform into sweet nuts, even in cooler regions. These nuts are often preferred over all others. The crinkled leaves are densely packed, making it an ideal hedge. The further south macadamias are planted, the more sun is needed for the fruit to ripen.

CZ 10-12 HZ 4-12   Slow
10m ↔ 8m   Feb-Apr

Ficus microcarpa hillii

Extensively planted in Sydney, it resembles an airy, light-green leaved Moreton Bay fig. Clips and hedges readily. In colder southern zones it is the ultimate replacement for eucalypts. This tree provides cool shade 10°C cooler at 40°C than under a eucalypt, dense shade and glossy, fire-retardant leaves.

CZ 9b-13 HZ 4-8   Slow
15m ↔ 15m

Macadamia

Kaffir Plum

Harpephyllum syn. caffrum — Kaffir plums are an outstanding drought tolerant, rainforest evergreen from Africa. Their fast growth, neat form and shady habit make this fire-retardant tree an excellent choice in large gardens.

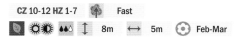
CZ 10-12 HZ 1-7   Fast
8m ↔ 5m   Feb-Mar

Flindersia australis

Australian Teak or Crow's Ash are names that celebrate its exceptional timber quality. It provides dense shade with ash-like leaves in dry areas, impressive white flowers and intriguing seed capsules. A spectacular specimen in the Adelaide Botanic Garden thrives in the driest heat.

CZ 9b-13 HZ 4-8   Medium
15m ↔ 10m   Feb-Mar

Ficus microcarpa hillii

Planting a tree

Australian Red Cedar

Kaffir Plum

Lilly Pilly

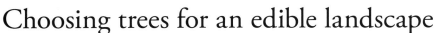

Choosing trees for an edible landscape

There are an extraordinary range of trees that provide either fruit or nuts with handsome form and good shade.

However some are untidy (like plums), too vigorous (like cherries), or need multiple plantings for cross pollination.

Here is a selection that gives you elegant shaped fruit trees, and good autumn colour for the right climate. Be sure to include these in your planting so your garden is both productive and beautiful.

We've refined the options so use this selector to create your own edible landscape.

Sub-tropical Gardens CZ 10-12

Banana Dwarf Cavendish

Musa acuminata — Bananas will grow and fruit in Cold Zone 10 but they are slower to grow in this zone than in Cold Zones 11 and 12. The plant to use for creating the tropical look, Cavendish is only 2.2m tall so it's less likely to be torn by the wind. A true herbaceous, self-pollinating perennial that needs fertile soil and heat.

CZ 10-13 HZ 4-13 Fast
☀✿ ▲▲◊ ↕ 2.2m ↔ 2m ◯ Feb-Mar

Macadamia

Macadamia tetraphylla — A popular Australian contribution to the international food scene. Tassels of ornamental pink flowers transform into sweet nuts. Crinkled leaves are densely packed, making an ideal hedge. The further south macadamias are planted the more sun is needed for the fruit to ripen.

CZ 10-12 HZ 4-12 Slow
☀✿ ▲▲◊ ↕ 10m ↔ 8m ◯ Feb-Apr

Babaco/Champagne Fruit

Carica pentagonia — This is the plant to create the typical tropical look in the sub-tropics with paw paw-like leaves. Huge 20-25cm yellow fruit with white flesh hang from the stem rather than the branches. Fast growing in fertile soils and full sun.

CZ 10-12 HZ 4-12 Fast
☀ ▲▲◊ ↕ 2.5m ↔ 1.5m ◯ Nov-Mar

Mango Kensington Pride

Mangifera indica — 'Mango Madness' is a condition that has described the anticipation of the wait for this fruit. A handsome evergreen that needs temperatures over 5°C at flowering time to produce fruit, making it suitable for Perth, Brisbane and further north. The perfect backyard tree for a sunny and fertile site in gardens with warm winters. Self-pollinating.

CZ 10-13 HZ 4-14 Medium
☀ ▲▲◊ ↕ 15m ↔ 6m ◯ Nov-Jan

Babaco

Coastal Frost Free Gardens CZ 10

Olive

Olea europaea — Olives capture the imagination with their old, gnarled trunks and silvery leaves shimmering in the wind amongst the Tuscan landscape. Evergreen, drought tolerant and with a 25% oil content, Frantoio has been the preferred variety for oil for centuries.

CZ 9a-11 HZ 1-10 Medium
☀ ▲▲◊ ↕ 6m ↔ 5m ◯ Apr-May

Avocado Hass

Persea americana — Thrives in every capital city except Canberra and Hobart, where it is too cold. Avocados are fast growing evergreens that will grow wherever camellias grow and who wouldn't swap winter blooms for 200 delicious fruit! In southern states, Hass will self pollinate, with fruit developing in spring and holding on the tree until needed. Fruit turns black when ready to eat. Prune in early summer to 2 metres.

CZ 10-11 HZ 4-9 Fast
☀ ▲▲◊ ↕ 10m ↔ 2m ◯ Sep-Jan

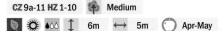

Olive

Banana

Pomegranate Elcite

Avocado Hass

Persimmon Ichikikei Jiro

Orange Navel Cara Cara

Citrus sinensis — It is worth planting an orange tree in the garden just for its foliage and the scent of orange blossom that fills the air. Striking, bright orange fruit is offset by dark green leaves. A seedless variety with pink tinged flesh, this is the first orange of the season.

CZ 9b-11 HZ 4-7   Slow

🍃 ☀ 💧 ↕ 2m ↔ 2m ◯ Aug-Oct

Fig St Dominique Violette

Ficus carica — One of my most memorable summer lunches was under the shade of a venerable fig. Just the right amount of shade and light enough to feel enclosed and intimate. This large leafed purple skinned fig has been a favourite for the last 140 years.

CZ 8-11 HZ 3-10   Medium

🍃 ☀ 💧 ↕ 3m ↔ 4m ◯ Feb-May

Lemon Verna

Citrus limon — One of the delights of visiting Cyprus in spring is the lemon blossom that permeates across the entire island. Verna is a reliable summer cropper with seedless flesh, unlike other varieties, and an acidic flavour – just when you need your cooling gin and tonic!

CZ 9b-11 HZ 4-11   Medium

🍃 ☀ 💧 ↕ 2.5m ↔ 2m ◯ Sep-Feb

Lemon

Frosty Winter Gardens CZ 8-9b

Persimmon Ichikikei Jiro

Diospyros kaki — Persimmons are the most beautiful of all fruiting trees. The graceful small stature is about citrus-size, with large, rounded foliage that produces spectacular autumn tones. Interest continues long into the season, with the orange fruit hanging on bare branches.

CZ 7-10 HZ 3-9   Medium

🍃 ☀ 💧 ↕ 5m ↔ 3m ◯ Mar-Apr

Pear Conference

Pyrus communis — The French adore pears and for all the right reasons. Worth planting just for its blossom alone. Elegantly shaped and first grown in 1885, Conference has elongated fruit, sweet melting flesh and stores well. Self fertile.

CZ 7-10 HZ 1-6   Medium

🍃 ☀ 💧 ↕ 3m ↔ 3m ◯ Mar-Apr

Apple Macintosh

Malus domestica — Flower buds of pink and white set the bees buzzing in spring, with burgundy coloured, scented fruit to follow. Macintosh is self-pollinating and a good partner for other apples. Look for dwarfing rootstock.

CZ 7-10 HZ 1-7   Medium

🍃 ☀ 💧 ↕ 3m ↔ 3m ◯ Mar-Apr

Pomegranate Elcite

Punica granatum — These glossy leafed shrubs put on a show of powder puff-red flowers in late spring and baubles of red fruit in late autumn. Elcite stands out from the crowd with striking yellow skin and glorious autumn colour.

CZ 9b-11 HZ 4-12   Medium

🍃 ☀ 💧 ↕ 4m ↔ 2m ◯ Feb-Apr

Blueberry

Vaccinium corymbosum — Thriving in the same conditions as azaleas and rhododendrons, enjoy the pink flowers in spring, blue fruit in summer and red tones of the foliage in autumn. Reveille has an excellent flavour.

CZ 8-10 HZ 1-6   Slow

🍃 ☀ 💧 ↕ 2.4m ↔ 2m ◯ Dec-Mar

Espalier Pear

Espalier Apple

Blueberry

Orange Navel Cara Cara

Small tree selector

White Cape Chestnut

Luma apiculata

Kapok

Snow Pear

Snow Pear

Pyrus nivalis — The silver leafed pear is really tough and is one of the most beautiful of all pears. Single white flowers appear in spring, followed by grey leaves. Drought tolerant.

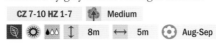
CZ 7-10 HZ 1-7 · Medium · 8m ↔ 5m · Aug-Sep

Cape Chestnut

Calodendrum capense — With glossy, deep green leaves and fragrant spikes of pink or white, this tree lights up the summer sky and cools the dry ground on hot days. Hailing from Africa, Cape Chestnuts are beautiful summer flowering trees that drop their leaves in cool winters.

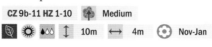
CZ 9b-11 HZ 1-10 · Medium · 10m ↔ 4m · Nov-Jan

Chinese Elm UMBRELLA FORM

Ulmus parvifolia — The best elm for hot, dry climates. Its umbrella growth habit provides maximum shade. The bark is striking, with orange and brown markings. Leaves fall after turning yellow or red. Excellent drought tolerance.

CZ 7-11 HZ 1-10 · Fast · 10m ↔ 20m

Kapok

Ceiba speciosa (syn. Chorisia speciosa) — Kapoks are the perfect choice for a city courtyard, where their rapid growth suddenly stops to create a living sculpture of spines and elegant fingered leaves. If left to grow in humid tropical areas, its orchid pink flowers eventually form fluffy cotton-like seed pods, that can be used for stuffing pillows.

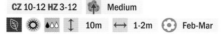
CZ 10-12 HZ 3-12 · Medium · 10m ↔ 1-2m · Feb-Mar

Jelly Palm

Butia capitata — Grey leaved palms stand out but this rare feathery palm produces delicious edible fruits too. The orange fruit is a blend of cherry and pineapple flavour.

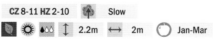
CZ 8-11 HZ 2-10 · Slow · 2.2m ↔ 2m · Jan-Mar

Russian Olive

Elaeagnus angustifolia — Grey foliage is ideal for highlighting areas of drab, green plantings. The Russian olive's sweeping form is faster to grow than the weeping pear, of which the British are obsessed, and has appealing fragrant yellow flowers. It is also much faster to grow than the common olive. Grows in areas with less than 250mm rainfall.

CZ 7-10 HZ 3-8 · Fast · 6m ↔ 8m · Sep-Oct

Podocarpus gracilor

In California, this fern-like pine is clipped to shape just like Irish yew, but its greener colour makes a better choice, plus it copes with the heat and grows faster. Left unpruned it is drought tolerant, evergreen, graceful and doesn't make a mess in the garden.

CZ 9a-12 HZ 3-10 · Medium · 5m ↔ 2m

Luma apiculata

From the southern hemisphere, this is a relative of our eucalypts. It has cinnamon coloured, peeling bark, white flowers in summer and beautiful evergreen glossy leaves. An ideal choice for gardeners that don't want to plant inflammable eucalyptus, and it also makes a good hedge.

CZ 9b-11 HZ 4-11 · Medium · 8m ↔ 5m · Dec-Jan

Black Locust

Robinia pseudoacacia — This drought proof and fast growing tree produces the hardest of fence posts. It is the tree for every farm where its successors or seeds don't take over. Grown on non-suckering root stocks and pollarded, Robinias are planted all through rural France to show off their flowers of white, pink or purple and their elegant leaves.

CZ 7-11 HZ 1-10 · Fast · 10m ↔ 6m · Oct-Nov

Chinese Elm

Jelly Palm

Russian Olive

Podocarpus gracilor

Tall tree selector NUTS & FRUIT

Stone Pine

Mulberry Shahtoot

Chestnut

Pecan

Walnut ENGLISH

Walnut ANDEAN

Sugar Maple

Mulberry

Our Mulberry tree in the Heronswood valley is over 100 years old, probably a cutting from Georgiana McCrae's homestead down the hill. Easy to grow, its gnarled trunk looks old early and it is an excellent, fast growing shade tree with golden autumn leaves.

* BLACK MULBERRY *Morus nigra* — With flavour as good as blackberry but fruit so sweet and soft it doesn't reach the market. Fruits in time for Christmas. ↕ 8m ↔ 12m

* WHITE MULBERRY *Morus alba* — Fruit lacks acid with leaves that feed silk worms. A first rate ornamental tree. ↕ 4m ↔ 4m

* SHAHTOOT *Morus macroura* — Elongated sweet fruit. ↕ 5m ↔ 5m

CZ 7-11 HZ 1-8 Fast

☀ ◊◊◊ Nov-Jan

Pecan

Carya illinoinensis — Superior eating to walnuts, the pecan has over 500 different selections. Fast growing, it loves the heat, moisture and deep soils for its long tap root. A truly outstanding deciduous tree with golden autumn leaves. The Shoshoni variety has large nuts.

CZ 7-10 HZ 5-8 Fast

☀ ◊◊◊ ↕ 30m ↔ 12m Mar-May

Sugar Maple

Acer saccharum — The "Maple Syrup" maple is one of the reasons tourists flock to Canada and the US east coast. The mid green leaves turn yellow in autumn and the sap, the source of maple syrup, is harvested in spring.

CZ 7-10 HZ 1-5 Fast

☀ ◊◊◊ ↕ 15m ↔ 6m

Stone Pine

Pinus pinea — This umbrella-shaped pine is Italy's favourite shade tree, often pruned to an upward single trunk. We have an avenue where the precious nuts, used for pesto, have formed in less than 10 years. This is the iconic pine that features on all Tuscan postcards.

* WALKER — This selection holds its pine nuts until it drops to the ground to protect from birds.

CZ 8-11 HZ 1-10 Fast

☀ ◊◊◊ ↕ 15m ↔ 10m Mar-May

Chestnut

Castanea sativa — Fast growing with tasty, low-fat nuts, tree expert Hugh Johnson describes Chestnuts as a spectacular "billowing pyramid of light catching leaves". The furrowed trunks are known to have reached 60 metres round.

CZ 7-10 HZ 1-8 Fast

☀☀ ◊◊◊ ↕ 15m ↔ 10m Apr-Jun

Walnut

Julgans sp. — Excellent shade trees that produces incredibly expensive timber. The nuts crop all through winter and are perfect to crack before the fire. Walnuts need good, deep soils.

* ANDEAN *J. neotropica* — Evergreen. Self-pollinating crop of smaller nuts and darker timber. ↕ 15m ↔ 10m Fast

* ENGLISH *J. regia* — Deciduous. Self-pollinating tree with oval nuts. ↕ 15m ↔ 10m Medium

CZ 7-10 HZ 1-7

☀ ◊◊◊ ↕ 15m ↔ 10m Mar-May

Oak ENGLISH

Oak SCARLET

Oak HOLM

Desert Ash

Argentine Ombu

Himalayan Cedar

Maidenhair Tree

Oak CORK

Maidenhair Tree

Ginkgo biloba — *Is it a native if this ancient tree has leaf fossils found in rocks in central Australia?* Native fanatics ignore that the ginkgo evolved as a conifer before continents drifted apart 150 million years ago. Whilst classified a conifer, it looks like the most elegant broad leaf with maidenhair-like leaves that turn a spectacular autumn yellow; a rare sight in frost free areas.

CZ 7-10 HZ 1-10

 20m ↔ 5m Slow

Oak

Quercus sp. — Is there a more stoic tree to protect your house from bushfires, a shady place when temperatures reach 40°C or a better legacy for any tree planted since colonisation? Both English and Holm oaks are symbiotic for truffle production.

- ENGLISH *Q. robur* — Chartreuse foliage in spring, fissured grey brown bark with deep water seeking tap root. ↕ 15m ↔ 12m ◳ Deciduous.

- CORK *Q. suber* — The spongy bark that is used to cork wine bottles is also a living sculpture. Grey-green evergreen leaves. Exceptionally drought tolerant. ↕ 8m ↔ 6m ◳ Evergreen.

- HOLM *Q. ilex* — Holly-like leaves are a dark foliage contrast that hedge beautifully. Left to grow it is the dominant evergreen in Italy which is an elegant contrast to other green trees. Exceptionally drought tolerant. ↕ 12m ↔ 8m ◳ Evergreen.

- SCARLET *Q. coccinea* — A blaze of intensely crimson leaves with jagged outline. ↕ 12m ↔ 8m ◳ Deciduous.

CZ 7-10 HZ 1-9

 20m ↔ 5m Medium

Argentine Ombu

Phytolacca dioica — This corpulent tree has the biggest girth and is a botanic sculpture. In every farm or school it would be welcome as a kids playground and imagine how much money that would save!

Cooling green leaves provide excellent shade and huge specimens found on farms testify to its survival of droughts, bush fires and heat waves.

CZ 9b-12 HZ 4-11 🌲 Fast

 8m ↔ 16m

Desert Ash

Fraxinus augustifolia supsp. oxycarpa — Tired of arid inflammable eucalypts? This tough survivor could shelter 400 wedding guests from the sun (10° cooler than a eucalypt) on Heronswood's main lawn.

Its branches are horizontal and its new spring leaf growth is chartreuse then yellow in autumn. The pick for shade in the arid zones (see photograph on pages 126-127).

CZ 7-10 HZ 1-8

 15m ↔ 25m Medium

Himalayan Cedar

Cedrus deodara — The most majestic of conifers with horizontal see-through branches, beautiful cones, handsome bark and deep green aromatic needles.

Needs space and features in the gardens of period dramas set in Australia and the UK.

CZ 7-10 HZ 1-8

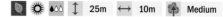 25m ↔ 10m Medium

Ephemeral bulbs

Bulbs are precious jewels of flowers: they are impressive and hugely decorative, but they are the ephemera of the flowering world, most appearing for no more than two weeks a year.

The famous carpets of colour that attract millions of visitors to Keukenhof in the Netherlands every spring are quite bare after flowering and for the rest of the year.

Bulbs are best planted with other companions and not alone in their own feature beds. They provide delicious seasonal highlights, but they are the souffle, never the main course: once the souffle collapses, the empty dish is bare and forlorn.

Bulbs flower so briefly that a garden planted with bulbs alone can be a huge disappointment.

Mature gardeners learn to raise bulbs as the entree or dessert, and organise the main course using shrubs and perennials, which provide year-round form and structure.

Most bulbs have been bred for the cut flower market because flowering is too brief to justify placement in a garden.

The bulbs that suit planting in a garden are best naturalised under trees or shrubs so they don't need replanting, or planted within flower borders, like liliums that flower in summer and die down in winter so they can be left undisturbed.

TOP Keukenhof, Holland, ▶ March/April. Australian equivalent is Sep-Oct only.

RIGHT Tulips combined with muscari.

BOTTOM LEFT Liliums, best planted in summer borders.

BOTTOM RIGHT Tall beech.

Bulbs for naturalising

Spanish Blue Bells

Spring flowering

Almost all the bulbs grown in Australia come from lands with a similar Mediterranean climate, with tulips coming from Turkey, daffodils from Spain and Portugal and gladiolus from South Africa. They thrive in climates with cold winters, wet springs and dry summers so that, once planted, they fit the natural rhythm of our seasonal changes with minimal attention.

They are as safe as a plant can be because most bulbs are a natural storage organ with the flowers already formed in the dormant bulb. As summer temperatures cool and autumn rains commence the roots grow down and the leaves shoot up ready to produce some of the most sought after flowers for cutting.

They have but one weakness: a shortness of flowering followed by unsightly foliage making them unsuitable for summer borders or anywhere where one is regularly digging.

But they grow to perfection around the base of shrubs, naturalised amongst trees or throughout a lawn. All bulbs need good drainage and, for best effect, plant clumps of 5–20 bulbs rather than solitary plantings.

They are a novice gardener's dream thriving in the driest conditions and surviving the hottest summers given adequate spring moisture and some can even be grown in the tropics if you are prepared to lift after flowering.

Star Flower

Grape Hyacinth PEPPERMINT

Grape Hyacinth PINK SUNRISE

Spring flowering

Spanish Blue Bells

Hyacinthoides hispanica — A carpet of blue before deciduous trees and shrubs burst into leaf. Naturalise in shady, damp soils. White and pink forms create a well blended mix.

CZ 7-10 HZ 1-8

☀☀ ⬥⬥ ↕ 30cm ↔ 8cm ⊚ Sep-Nov

Star Flower

Ipheion uniflorum — Blue stars face heavenwards and naturalise in the Heronswood lawn provided dying foliage is not mown until November. The scent of garlic and their blue colour suits under-planting in rose beds too. Flowers in pale blue, white and violet.

CZ 7-11 HZ 1-8

☀☀ ⬥⬥ ↕ 10cm ↔ 3cm ⊚ Jul-Sep

Tritonia PINK

Scilla peruviana subsp. hughii

Smokey lilac, dome-like flower heads.

CZ 7-10 HZ 1-8

☀☀ ⬥⬥ ↕ 30cm ↔ 8cm ⊚ Sep-Nov

Freesias

* *Freesia alba* — Creamy short stemmed flowers with egg yolk colouration are deliciously fragrant thriving in dry, sandy bare areas. ↕ 15m ↔ 8cm
* FLORIST HYBRIDS — Tall stems for cutting come in hideous mixed colours of white, purple, red and yellow, so select single colours for planting. ↕ 20m ↔ 5cm

CZ 9-11 HZ 1-11 ☀ ⬥⬥ ⊚ Sep-Oct

Grape Hyacinth

Muscari armeniacum — Enlarged flower spikes are charming massed in clumps and left to naturalise. Blue, white and pink colours.

CZ 7-11 HZ 1-8

☀☀ ⬥⬥ ↕ 20cm ↔ 5cm ⊚ Sep

Tritonia flabollifolia var. *major*

Similar to ixias, with wiry stems but open, large blooms. Good for cutting and naturalising in a dry, sunny spot.

CZ 7-10 HZ 1-8

☀☀ ⬥⬥ ↕ 30cm ↔ 5cm ⊚ Oct-Nov

Grape Hyacinth

Scilla peruviana subsp. hughii

Freesia alba

Peacock Iris

Naturalised bulbs at Cloudehill

Ixia

One of the most striking and persistent wildflowers. Thrives in dry, sunny areas in hot yellows and reds.

- *Ixia maculata* — Orange petals with dark eyes. Also known as Corn Lily.
- BLUE *I. viridiflora* — Surreal jade-green colours with a central dark eye make this the most striking spring flower.

CZ 8-10 HZ 1-8

☀ ◔◔◔ ↕ 70cm ↔ 20cm ◉ Oct-Nov

Arum Lily

Zantedeschia aethiopica — Perfect for wet and boggy soils, their foliage and flowers are elegant and striking. Rapidly multiplying, tuberous rhizomes.

- GREEN GODDESS — White trumpets and green spathes.

CZ 9b-10 HZ 1-8

☀☀ ◔◔◔ ↕ 1.2m ↔ 60cm ◉ Jul-Oct

Dutch Crocus

Crocus vernus — Exquisite jewels of flowers that emerge in late winter in frosty areas. Recommended varieties are Pickwick, Grand Maitre and Joan of Arc.

CZ 9b-7 HZ 1-6

☀ ◔◔◔ ↕ 12cm ↔ 3cm ◉ Sep-Oct

Snowflakes

Leucojum aestivum — The poor man's snowdrop has nodding white bells with a green dot. Naturalises in grass that is avoided by animals. Leaves are flat like those of daffodils.

CZ 7-10 HZ 1-8

☀☀ ◔◔◔ ↕ 40cm ↔ 7cm ◉ Jul-Sep

Dutch Crocus JOAN OF ARC

Dutch Crocus PICKWICK

Ixia BLUE

Peacock Iris

Morea aristata — Delicate and enchanting and so aptly named, with snow-white petals and peacock eyes just for you. Flowering is brief but unforgettable. Be sure to plant in a prominent spot where this pop-up treasure will never be missed.

CZ 9a-10 HZ 1-7

☀ ◔◔◔ ↕ 50cm ↔ 10cm ◉ Sep-Nov

Arum Lily GREEN GODDESS

Snowflakes

Dutch Crocus YELLOW

137

Daffodils

Daffodils don't have to be yellow! There are pink, white and "greenish" daffodils and jonquil types with fragrant, multiple flowers giving them greater appeal as cut flowers. Daffodils that flower before September are best planted in lawns in groupings of 10 that can be mowed in late October without affecting next year's flowering. Late flowering bulbs are best grown in beds or under deciduous trees. Trumpet daffodils don't like warm winters so gardeners in the sub-tropics (CZ 10-11) should choose the jonquil non-trumpet types.

CZ 7-9b HZ 1-8 Aug-Sep

Daffodil garden at St Erth

King Alfred

Thalia MINI

Mabel Taylor

Hoop Petticoat MINI

King Alfred

Narcissus x tenuior — King Alfred is the common large yellow trumpet that heralds the beginning of spring. ↕ 25cm ↔ 10cm

Rus Holland

Narcissus x tenuior — The closest to a green daffodil with large trumpets and pale green cups. Bred by Hugh Dettman in 1969. ↕ 25cm ↔ 10cm

Mabel Taylor

Narcissus x tazetta — Probably the best pink trumpet daffodil with large white petals to highlight the pink edged corolla trumpet. Bred by Alister Clark. ↕ 30-70cm ↔ 10cm

Miniature daffodils

Hoop Petticoat

Narcissus bulbocodium — Perfect yellow petticoats of yellow cups. ↕ 15cm ↔ 3cm ☉ Sep

Thalia

Narcissus triandrus — 2-3 exquisite ivory-white flowers as delicate as the finest orchid. ↕ 30cm ↔ 20cm

How many bulbs?

Of course it depends on your pocket but even 3-5 bulbs planted closely together will look lonely until they multiply. You need clumps of 10-20 to create impact and 100 will certainly look eye-catching.

But remember, 100 bulbs planted 8cm apart will still only cover 1.6m². Best to plant minimum groups of 10-20 and expect the second and third year multiplication to create the impact.

Paper White

Moon Fairies

Geranium

Jonquils MULTI-HEADED

The choice for warm coastal areas like Sydney, Melbourne and Perth.

 CZ 7-10 HZ 1-8

Paper White

Narcissus papyraceus — Snow white star-shaped single flowers appear in early May, well before all other jonquils. ↕ 30cm ↔ 8cm ☉ May-Jun

Dickcissel

Narcissus jonquilla — A collector's passion. Reverse bicolour mini jonquil that starts yellow and fades to white. ↕ 50cm ↔ 8cm ☉ Aug-Sep

Geranium

Narcissus x tazetta — Up to six exceptionally fragrant white flowers and orange-red cups. ↕ 50cm ↔ 10cm ☉ Sep-Oct

Erlicheer

Narcissus x odorus — Creamy, yellow double flowers are beautifully scented. ↕ 40cm ↔ 10cm ☉ Jul-Aug

Moon Fairies

Narcissus x jonquilla — Fairy-like yellow dainty daffodils are a mini multi-headed version of King Alfred. ↕ 30cm ↔ 10cm ☉ Sep-Oct

Soleil d'Or

N. tazetta — The second earliest golden yellow with orange cup is highly fragrant. ↕ 20cm ↔ 10cm ☉ Jun-Jul

Pheasants Eye

N. poeticus — The latest to flower. Just after the snow melts *poeticus* daffodils burst into flower and cover whole meadows leaving an indelible memory. Elegant white arching flowers with a yellow corolla with red edging. ↕ 30cm ↔ 8cm ☉ October

Pheasants Eye

Soleil d'Or

Dickcissel

Erlicheer

Bulbs to grow in the cutting garden

Tulip SPRING GREEN

Anemone de Caen

Gladiolus tristis

Ranunculus

Tulip ANGELIQUE

Tulip CRYSTAL BEAUTY

Tulip MIXED

Tulip

Tulipa sp. — Literally thousands of cultivars have been developed in Holland over 400 years since Turkish bulbs were first cross bred. If given 8 weeks winter chilling at 5 degrees or less when soil temperature fall below 14 degrees they may naturalise. Otherwise, plant as annuals.

CZ 7-9b HZ 1-7

   40cm ↔ 10cm ⊚ Sep-Nov

Anemone de Caen

Anemone coronaria — Like giant single poppies with black centres and parsley-like foliage. Flowers in blue, white, red and bicolours. They are grown as annuals in March, with the corms planted point down. Single flowers are more charming than doubles.

CZ 7-11 HZ 1-12

     50cm ↔ 5cm ⊚ Aug-Oct

Gladiolus sp.

Early summer flowers for the vase don't suit garden planting except for some true perennial clumping forms.

- THE BRIDE — Pure white. ↕ 60cm ↔ 5cm
- *G. murielae* — Very fragrant.
  ↕ 70cm ↔ 15cm
- *G. tristis* — Jade green fragrant flowers.
  ↕ 60cm ↔ 5cm

CZ 9a-11 HZ 1-12  ⊚ Nov-Dec

Ranunculus

Ranunculus x asiaticus — These doubles often look hideous with pinks and yellows clashing with reds and whites. Choose single colours and grow like anemones with claw-like corms planted point down.

CZ 8-11 HZ 1-12

    30cm ↔ 5cm ⊚ Sep-Nov

Tulip CHARMEUR

Bulbs for garden beds SPRING FLOWERING

Russian Garlic

Veltheimia LEMON

Veltheima bracteata

Veltheimia bracteata

One of the pleasures of gardening in a hotter drier gardening climate is growing exquisite plants the English cannot. This South African native deserves to be grown wherever hellebores and clivias thrive. Strap-like wavy green leaves launch pendant tubes of exceptionally rare pale yellow or purplish pink.

CZ 10-12 HZ 1-7

 45cm 30cm Aug-Oct

Allium

These pop-up tubular flowers fit perfectly in perennial flower gardens adding vertical visuals that can be left undisturbed to rapidly multiply.

* BLUE DRUMSTICK *A. caeruleum* — Round heads of smokey blue appear in spring. 60cm 10cm

* DRUMSTICK *A. sphaerocephalum* — Striking globes of chive-like flower heads start green opening to burgundy. 90cm 10cm

* STAR OF PERSIA *A. cristophii* — Huge metallic pink globes. 50cm 20cm

CZ 7-10 HZ 1-8 Nov-Dec

Pineapple Lily Purple

Eucomis comosa — With its creamy star-shaped flowers and pineapple-like stems, the Pineapple Lily has darker green-purple contrasting leaves which provide good foliage contrast whilst flowering all summer long.

CZ 8-12 HZ 1-12

 80cm 30cm Jan-Mar

Russian Garlic

Allium ampeloprasum — This is a cross over "ornamental edible" with tall, very large allium flowers and bulbs that are coarser than true garlic but have a mild sweet flavour. Long lived bulbs naturalise in hot sandy areas. Just the plant for the back of a border. Lift 4-5cm cloves in autumn if needed.

CZ 7-10 HZ 1-6

 1.5m 30cm Oct-Nov

Pineapple Lily PURPLE

Allium BLUE DRUMSTICK

Allium STAR OF PERSIA

Allium DRUMSTICK

Bulbs for garden beds

Lilium leucanthum

Madonna Lily

Lilium nepalense

Liliums

Dreamy perfume scents the summer air but the common Christmas Lily has lots of relatives that are spectacular summer flowers to be planted in a border and left to multiply.

* MADONNA LILY *L. candidum* — Purest white symbol of chastity scents the air in late spring. Must have alkaline soil. ↕ 1.5m ↔ 50cm ☉ Nov-Jan

* *L. nepalense* — This is the bulb equivalent of the blue poppy. Lime-green petals reflex open to maroon – an amazing colour combination. Stoloniferous spreading of bulbs that thrive in humus rich, moist soils and produce a heady evening fragrance. ↕ 1m ↔ 40cm ☉ Feb-Mar **CZ 7-9b HZ 1-6**

* *L. leucanthum var. centifolium* — Exceptionally fragrant yellow throated trumpets with purple stripes on outside petals. ↕ 2m ↔ 40cm ☉ Feb-Mar

* TIGER LILY *L. lancifolium* — Tiger coloured with spotted trumpets hang and petals reflex open. ↕ 1.2m ↔ 30cm ☉ Jan-Feb

* *L. philippinense* — Magnificent early autumn pure white fragrant trumpets. ↕ 1m ↔ 30cm

CZ 9a-11 HZ 1-10 🍃 ☀ 💧

Fairy's Fishing Rods

Dierama pulcherrimum — Gently arching stems wave with graceful bell-shaped flowers in early summer. Available in white, pink or beetroot colour.

CZ 9a-11 HZ 1-10 🍃 ☀ 💧 ↕ 1.5m ↔ 50cm ☉ Dec-Jan

Sea Squill

Drimia maritima — With towering leafless stems, somewhat like *Eremurus* that emerge from large belladonna-like bulbs that naturalise in hot, dry climates.

CZ 9b-10 HZ 4-8 🍃 ☀ 💧 ↕ 90cm ↔ 15m ☉ Mar-Apr

Belladonna Lily

Amaryllis belladonna — Well named "Naked Ladies" appear on long stems, yet to be clothed by large strap-like leaves. Bulbs naturalise into huge sized clumps. With 4-12 trumpet-like flowers per stem, Belladonna lily is fragrant and tough in full sun. Available in white, light pink, dark pink and the most precious and hard to find blue, *Worsleya procera*.

CZ 8-11 HZ 1-10 🍃 ☀☀ 💧 ↕ 45cm ↔ 30m ☉ Feb-Mar

Sea Squill

Tiger Lily

Belladonna Lily PINK

Fairy's Fishing Rod PINK

Belladonna Lily WHITE

Fairy's Fishing Rod WHITE

Autumn flowering

Hardy Cyclamen

Blood Lily

Nerine WHITE

Nerine PINK

Most Australian gardens are flat and dull after our summer. But many bulbs from South Africa's *Amaryllis* family (blood lilies, belladonna, nerine, *Hippeastrum*), have adapted to the summer dry by resting and flowering in time for the autumn rains. Truly spectacular and enchanting flowers appear often followed by leaves to generate energy for next year's flowering.

Rain Lily

Zephyranthes candida — These "look at me" starry flowers emerge after rain multiplying rapidly in subtropics with onion-like leaves.

CZ 9-11 HZ 2-12

 10cm ↔ 3cm 🌣 Jan-Apr

Hardy Cyclamen

C. hederifolium — This frost hardy cyclamen, with its shorter stem and magically reflexed petals, has marbled leaves that emerge from grapefruit-sized bulbs. One of autumn's most memorable sights.

CZ 8-10 HZ 1-7

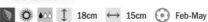 18cm ↔ 15cm 🌣 Feb-May

Autumn Crocus

Colchicum lusitanum — Rosy mauve goblets remind us of shortening days before long ribbed leaves develop. Good for pots or in front of shrubs.

CZ 7-11 HZ 1-6

 15cm ↔ 10cm 🌣 Mar

Blood Lily

Haemanthus coccineus — The most intriguing bulb with huge 10cm strappy autumn flowering curved leaves that emerge after naked flowering. The red paintbrush flowers push through clam-like lips of a huge above ground bulb. Easily naturalises and its foliage is a striking ground cover in dry shade.

- WHITE BLOOD LILY *H. albiflos* — White form.

CZ 9b-10 HZ 1-6

 25cm ↔ 30cm 🌣 Mar-Apr

Nerine

With wavy re-curved petals and strap-like leaves, this delight is best left to naturalise to lift the beauty of your autumn garden.

- WHITE *Nerine undulata* — When massed, this is as memorable as Wordsworth's poem about a host of garden daffodils *"beside the lake, beneath the trees, fluttering and dancing in the breeze"*.
- RED AND PINK *N. sarniensis*

CZ 8-10 HZ 1-10

 40cm ↔ 30cm 🌣 Apr-Jun

Yellow Spider Lily

Lycoris aurea — Leafless stems appear adorned with golden, spider-like tendrils.

CZ 8-10 HZ 1-10

 30cm ↔ 50cm 🌣 Jan-Feb

Spider Lily YELLOW

Rain Lily

Autumn Crocus

Cosmos YELLOW

Nasturtium ALASKA GOLD

Ephemeral annuals for direct sowing

Growing annuals from seed has been going out of favour over the last 50 years, as professional seedling growers offer punnets of already germinated dwarf plants. Regrettably this has removed from our gardens some of the most charming flowers for a cottage garden.

We urge you to think again by planting easy-to-germinate, quick growing annuals that will create more appealing garden pictures than anything available as modern bedding in seedling form.

HA HARDY ANNUALS — Frost hardy flowers that germinate in 10-15°C soil and flower in about 3 months before excessive heat.

TA TENDER ANNUALS — Tender annuals mostly come from the frost free tropics of Mexico or South America and need 20°C+ soil temperatures to germinate and can't tolerate cold autumn or spring temperatures below 15°C, flowering through summer and autumn (or year round in tropics).

Planting timetable for annuals

	Spring flowering, hardy annuals	Summer flowering, tender annuals
Sow	Feb-Mar	Aug-Sep
Soil temp.	10-15°C	20°C+
Flowering	Aug-Nov	Jan-Apr
Remove and dig over	November	April

◄ TOP Natural cottage flowers.

MIDDLE This annual bedding display in Europe is planted as a diverse grouping, not a mono-culture as in American bedding. The look is natural and grey foliage lightens the blobs of colour.

BOTTOM This ghastly photo from an American plant breeder shows that all the modern flowers are bred down to be at ankle height – called bedding annuals.

Direct sow tender annuals in spring for summer flowering

Pink Cleome

White Cosmos with blue Salvia

Cosmos PINKIE

Cleome

C. spinosa — Some call it the Spider Flower but Cat's Whiskers seems more accurate. Beloved by bees for its length of flowering, even its seed pods are appealing, extending interest for months. Up to 1m tall. Fast growing, purple, white and pink flowers.

TA ☀ ⬤⬤⬤ ↕ 1.5m ↔ 60cm ◉ Dec-Mar

Love Lies Bleeding

Amaranthus caudatus — The French call it "the foxtail" with its blood red colour but it also has edible leaves and its seeds provide the superfood cereal amaranth.

TA ☀ ⬤⬤⬤ ↕ 1m ↔ 80cm ◉ Feb-Mar

Cosmos

Happy, unsophisticated daisies that flower quickly and for a long period in late spring after the last frost sowing or all through summer. Hardier than most tender annuals it combines beautifully with salvias or blue agastache. We prefer single, unadulterated varieties to the semi-doubles.

- YELLOW *C. bipinnatus* — The white single cosmos that changes colour to yellow with the shortening autumn days. ↕ 1m ↔ 80cm
- *C. sulphureus* — The shorter semi-double with spidery leaves and everlasting orange, yellow and red flowers. ↕ 70cm ↔ 50cm

TA ☀ ⬤⬤⬤ ◉ Sep-Mar

Gaillardia

G. pulchella — Thriving during extreme hot summers when all else fails, the double flowers dazzle with toned down gold, purple-reds and burgundy. Long flowering.

TA ☀ ⬤⬤⬤ ↕ 40cm ↔ 20cm ◉ Dec-Mar

Four O'Clock

Mirabilis jalapa — Imagine a tuberous plant that opens its flowers for afternoon tea, lasting through dinner to breakfast. Exceptionally fragrant, tiny trumpet-like flowers splashed with broken colours of white, yellow and red that can actually change colours from white to violet, yellow to pink. It's child's play to grow.

TP ⬤⬤⬤ ☀ ↕ 50cm ↔ 30cm ◉ Dec-Mar

Quinoa

Chenopodium quinoa — Pronounced 'keen-wah'. Originating in the Andes, it's one of the few broad leafed plants that provides edible seeds, good foliage and handsome yellow cream and bronze flowers. Seeds have a coating that protect them from bird damage, and they contain high levels of essential amino acids, calcium and iron – it is exceptional compared to other grains.

TA ☀ ⬤⬤⬤ ↕ 1.7m ↔ 80cm ◉ Feb-Mar

Gaillardia

Four O'Clock

Quinoa

Love Lies Bleeding

Moonflower

Rudbeckia CHERRY BRANDY

Morning Glory HEAVENLY BLUE

Marigold RED MARIETTA

Marigold NAUGHTY MARIETTA

Marigold LEMON GEM

Clary Sage

Pincushion

Zinnia PURITY AND ENVY

Zinnia CALIFORNIAN GIANTS

Clary Sage

Salvia virdis — Cultivated in gardens since 1596, this salvia has the best and most agreeable colour range of all salvias. Its flowers are really sterile bracts that last well in spring and survive heat well to thrive through summer. Blue, pink, purple and white forms available. Half hardy.

TA HA ☀ ▲▲ ↕ 60cm ↔ 25cm ⊙ Dec-Mar

Salvia

S. farinacea — Most salvias are best grown as woody, drought tolerant shrubs, not for summer borders. But with long (longer than lavender), graceful spikes it is a foundation annual.

- BLUE BEDDER — Violet blue, long flowering spikes that contrast beautifully with single flowered cosmos, sunflowers, coneflowers or rudbeckias.
- WHITE BEDDER — Silvery-grey flower spikes.

TA ☀ ▲▲▲ ↕ 90cm ↔ 20cm ⊙ Dec-Mar

Pincushion

Scabiosa atropurpurea — Drought tolerance, long flowering and fragrance are surely enough to justify sowing. Its soft pincushion-like flowers are charming, particularly when naturalised and they make an excellent cut flower.

- BLACK KNIGHT — Deep maroon colour; often behaves as a perennial.
- MIXED — Blue, salmon, white and red.

TA ☀ ▲▲▲ ↕ 80cm ↔ 20cm ⊙ Dec-Mar

Moonflower

Ipomea alba — Why would you plant a climber that only flowered at night? Because as the luminous ghost-like blooms unfurl they are so fragrant you will want to call your friends over for a drink. Be sure to plant Four O'Clocks below to heighten the intensity.

TP ☀ ▲▲▲ ↕ 3m ↔ 120cm ⊙ Feb-Apr

Morning Glory Heavenly Blue

Ipomea tricolor — The glorious colour of Heavenly Blue is perfectly described. Flowering in just 6 weeks from sowing we create tripods for it to scale so our garden has vertical support for the most exquisite summer climber.

TA ☀ ▲▲ ↕ 2m ↔ 60cm ⊙ Dec-Mar

French Marigold

Tagetes erecta (syn. patuk) — *Does the American marigold (T. erecta) win the prize for the most vulgar flower to gain popularity in the last 50 years?* Far better to avoid the big, blousy doubles and polan the dainty French singles that flower endlessly in spring and summer. Attracts bees, repels pests — perfect for enlivening a vegie bed.

- NAUGHTY MARIETTA — Golden yellow with dark red, mahogany coloured eyes.
- RED MARIETTA — Dazzling red eyes on yellow petals.
- LEMON GEM *T. tenuifolia* — Profusion of tiny lemon flowers and scented fragrance.
- SWEET MACE *Tagetes lucida* — Mexican tarragon is so aromatic its anise-tarragon scent is as appealing as its tiny yellow, single flowers. Behaves as a perennial in frost-free area but flowers late-summer autumn.

TA ☀ ▲▲ ↕ 20cm ↔ 15cm ⊙ Oct-Mar

Zinnia

Z. elegans — These daisies thrive in ultra-hot summers of 30-35°C for 3-4 months at a time. Plant breeders have doubled the number of petals creating dahlia and chrysanthemum-like flower forms in every colour but blue.

- PURITY — White double. ↕ 80cm ↔ 50cm
- ENVY — Rare green colour, dahlia flowered semi-double. ↕ 80cm ↔ 50cm
- CALIFORNIAN GIANTS — Double flowers in red, yellow, orange and white. ↕ 1m ↔ 50cm

TA ☀ ▲▲ ⊙ Dec-Apr

Sunflowers

Sunflower ITALIAN WHITE

Sunflower VAN GOGH

Sunflowers

Helianthus annuus — Bees are mesmorised by the flowers, chooks produce excellent eggs, the Russians roast them like peanuts and children grow them to beat the world record. They reach flowering size earlier than almost any other flower (60 days), but not all make good garden plants. Choose multiple stem varieties for long lasting flower displays. Direct sow.

SINGLE FLOWER PER STEM

* GIANT RUSSIAN — Huge yellow plates of flower that win the tallest sunflower competitions then feed the chooks. Also an excellent wind break. ↕ 3m ↔ 50cm
* VAN GOGH'S LANDSCAPE — Mid-sized flowers for growing *en masse* (for conversion to margarine) that always stops the traffic. ↕ 1.5m ↔ 20cm

MULTIPLE FLOWERS PER STEM

* PRADO RED — Velvety mid-red. 10 heads per plant. ↕ 1.5m ↔ 40cm
* ITALIAN WHITE *H. debilis subsp. cucumerifolius* — Dark chocolate centres and multi-headed white flowers last for months. ↕ 1.4m ↔ 60cm

TA ☀ ▲▲◊ ✿ Oct-Mar

Snow on the Mountain

Euphorbia marginata — Its leaves are as cool as crushed ice with light green leaves edged with white.

* EARLY SNOW — Long day selection.

TA ☀ ▲◊◊ ↕ 1m ↔ 70cm ✿ Dec-Feb

> Our botanic gardens are the most overlooked sources of inspiration!

Sunflower MOONWALKER MULTI-STEM

Sunflower PRADO RED

Sunflower GIANT RUSSIAN

Snow on the Mountain

Giant Russian sunflower seeds

147

Direct sow hardy annuals in autumn for spring flowering

Californian Poppy CHAMPAGNE AND ROSES

Cornflower PINK

Cerinthe major

Cornflower DWARF BLUE

California Poppy SINGLE RED

Corncockle OCEAN PEARL

Californian Poppy SINGLE ORANGE

Corncockle LILAC

Californian Poppy JELLY BEANS

Alyssum Carpet of Snow

Lobularia maritima — This unassuming gem is continually in bloom with tiny, fragrant flowers that re-seed perpetually. A vital bee attractant to help pollinate fruit trees when grown as a ground cover. It will intensify rose fragrance planted beneath rose bushes as well as smother weeds and conserve soil moisture.

HA ☼☼ ●△△ ↕ 20cm ↔ 15cm ◉ All year

Californian Poppy

Eschscholzia californica — With an abundance of sun and light, no plant is more willing to cover the ground to spectacular effect with glaucous foliage and precocious flowering. It produces spectacular blooms in 8-10 weeks from sowing.

SINGLE VARIETIES

* CREAM — Single milky cream flowers
* ORANGE — The original wildflower
* RED CHIEF — Fire engine red flowers

DOUBLE VARIETIES

* JELLY BEANS — Double fluted bright red orange and pink
* CHAMPAGNE AND ROSES — Pale and darker pink fluted flowers

HA ☼ ●△△ ↕ 30cm ↔ 20cm ◉ Oct-Dec

Cornflower Dwarf Blue

Centaurea segetum — The cornflower was a common sight in cornfields (a term to describe fields that once grew oats and wheat) accompanied by Flanders poppy throughout Europe before selective herbicides wiped them out. A beautiful blue 5cm flower.

HA ☼ ●△△ ↕ 40cm ↔ 20cm ◉ Oct-Dec

Corncockle

Agrostemma githago — As eager to flower as cornflowers and Flanders poppy. Upward facing lilac or pure white flowers last for months.

HA ☼ ●△△ ↕ 80cm ↔ 20cm ◉ Oct-Dec

Cerinthe major

Too subtle for beginner gardeners, it has invaluable grey foliage and nodding purple bells that last all through the cooler months producing vital winter contrast.

HA ☼☼ ●△△ ↕ 70cm ↔ 35cm ◉ Sep-Nov

Love-in-a-Mist AFRICAN BRIDE

Love-in-a-Mist CURIOSITY

Meadow Daisy

Forget-Me-Not PINK

Forget-Me-Not BLUE AND WHITE

Calendula GREEN HEART ORANGE

Native Everlasting

Forget-Me-Not

Myositis alpestris — Yellow tulips with blue forget-me-nots, and pink tulips with white forget-me-nots are the most popular colour combinations. Sow to smother the weeds with exquisite light blue petals and yellow centres. Grown in blue or mixed colours. Hardy biennial.

B ☼☀ ♦♦◊ ↕ 40cm ↔ 40cm ⊙ Sep-Nov

Native Everlasting

Rhodanthe chlorocephala — The most willing of native wildflowers to spread their seeds far and wide from west to east coast. Everlasting paper-like flowers dry well but as a pinkish colour combination of massed display it is unforgettable.

HA ☼ ♦◊◊ ↕ 50cm ↔ 30cm ⊙ Oct-Dec

Calendula Green Heart Orange

Calendula officinalis — Named from the Latin *Kalenade* ("the first day of the month"') because it can be in flower every day of the year, opening usually at 9am. Elizabethans called it marigold before Mexico was discovered, which then became the source of the popular modern marigolds that took over. So willingly do they grow they barely need sowing. Edible petals.

HA ☼ ♦♦◊ ↕ 60cm ↔ 40cm ⊙ All year

Love-in-a-Mist

Nigella damascena — Of the easiest to cultivate, it naturalises readily and flowers freely in just 8 weeks. Five petalled flowers have a collar of thin, thread-like bracts.

* MISS JEKYLL — Sky blue double flowers.
* CURIOSITY *N. hispanica* — Violet blue flowers and spider-like seed pods.
* AFRICAN BRIDE *N. hispanica* — White with velvety black centres.

HA ☼ ♦◊◊ ↕ 30cm ↔ 30cm ⊙ Oct-Dec

Meadow Daisy

Bellis perennis — Carpets of snow white Daisies will turn your lawn into a meadow simply by over sowing your lawn in autumn. Perfect in lawns where mowing spreads the seeds and about 1/100th the price of planting daffodils. Hardy biennial.

B ☼☀ ♦♦◊ ↕ 5cm ↔ 5cm ⊙ Aug-Oct

Mistakes beginners make

Test after test proves seedlings transplanted in flower do not perform as well as those seedlings transplanted before they show colour!

The most common mistake first time gardeners make is to combine spring and summer annuals together. It is far better to separate the seeds like hardy annuals for autumn sowings and tender annuals for spring sowing.

Opium Poppy with Orlaya

Hollyhock BLACK

Shirley Poppy

Orlaya grandiflora

Poppy LADYBIRD

Shirley Poppy ANGELS CHOIR

Nasturtium EMPRESS OF INDIA

Poppy

Papaver sp. — Is there any flower more exciting to grow? Whilst flowering is brief, its form and colour are so engaging that it is always memorable. Each flower produces so much seed that once it sheds in dry sunny parts of a garden it naturalises.

- FLANDERS FIELD *P. rhoeas* — Flaming red with black blotch. ↕ 60cm ↔ 30cm

- SHIRLEY POPPY *P. rhoeas* — Reselection of Flanders Poppy to concentrate white, pink, lilac tones instead of red. ↕ 80cm ↔ 30cm

- LADYBIRD *P. rhoeas* — Conspicuous black dots on outside of petals of a darker Flanders red. ↕ 50cm ↔ 30cm

- ICELAND *P. nudicaule* — The best cut flower and most long flowering poppy. Wonderland mixture. ↕ 25cm ↔ 10cm

- OPIUM *P. somniferum* — The source of many wars and desperation is one of the most beautiful flowers, with exquisite dry salt-shaker pods. In black, red, purple, pink and white. ↕ 150cm ↔ 20cm

HA ☀ ♦♦♦ ⦿ Oct-Dec

Nasturtium

Tropaeolum minus — Shield-like leaves stand above fleshy stems with red or orange blood-like flowers like a trophy, hence the Latin name *Tropaeolum*. The piquantly pepper flavour of the flowers and leaves will transform any salad mix. The perfect hot colour mix for our vegetable garden as well as the easiest flower to grow!

- ALASKA — Green leaves splashed with white. Gold or scarlet flowers. ↕ 20cm ↔ 20cm

- TRAILING MIX *T. majus* — Red, yellow and orange flowered climber to cover a fence. ↕ 1.5m ↔ 1m

- EMPRESS OF INDIA — Dark leaves and deep red flowers. ↕ 20cm ↔ 20cm

TA ☀☀ ♦♦♦ ⦿ Autumn & Spring

Orlaya grandiflora

Queen Anne's lace, the wild carrot, crosses with culinary carrots and takes two seasons to flower, but orlaya is quicker and elegant with pristine white lacy flower plates above ferny foliage providing a see-through effect. Easy to grow.

HA ☀ ♦♦♦ ↕ 75cm ↔ 40cm ⦿ Oct-Dec

Nasturtium ALASKA VARIEGATED FOLIAGE

Nasturtium LADYBIRD

Canterbury Bells

Hollyhock HALO

Sweet Pea HIGHSCENT

Sweet Pea MATUCANA

Sweet Pea PAINTED LADY

Sweet Peas

Lathyrus odoratus — The original sweet pea had exquisite fragrance but small flowers; there after plant breeders selected for larger flowers until world famous breeder Charles Unwin remarked *"I never realized why sweet peas were so named"*, We prefer to capture the fragrance and the original appeal. ***To extend flowering two months later, sow in spring rather than autumn.***

SMALL FLOWERS FOR ULTIMATE FRAGRANCE

* MATUCANA — The most sweetly scented, sweet pea with bicolour flowers of magenta and purple.

* PAINTED LADY — First named in 1737, this sweet pea has a pink standard and very pale-pink wings below.

* HIGH SCENT — Antique cream colour of exceptional fragrance.

* HEAVENLY SCENTED — Mixture of blue, Painted Lady and Highscent.

HA ☀ ♦♦♦ ↕ 2m ↔ 50cm ⊙ Dec-Apr

Mignonette

Reseda odorata — Introduced in 1752 and hailed as one of the few flowers that *"possess a fragrance so delightful and distinctive"* (Pizzetti and Cocker). Minute vertical columns of cream coloured blooms appear in spring.

HA ☀☀ ♦♦♦ ↕ 30cm ↔ 20cm ⊙ Oct-Nov

Honesty

Lunaria annua — Rare and exquisite. Silver edged leaves are followed by purple flowers for 6-12 months then by lunar-like, translucent seed heads much sought after by florists. Hardy, self-seeding biennial, it does best in some shade.

B ☀ ♦♦♦ ↕ 70cm ↔ 50cm ⊙ Sep-Nov

Canterbury Bells

Campanula medium — In cultivation since 1597, this darling of English gardeners has the largest of campanula flowers but behaves as a biennial down under. Pink, white and blue colours harmonise as a mixture. Hardy biennial.

B ☀ ♦♦♦ ↕ 90cm ↔ 60cm ⊙ Sep-Nov

Hollyhock

Alcea rosea — So popular were hollyhocks in the 1870s, Vilmorin listed more than 80 varieties. Needing just sun and heat their long tap roots source water in dry soils whilst the flowers can reach 2.5m tall. *Hybrids that produce doubles are to be avoided.* Single flowers like lupins and delphiniums are foundation cottage garden plants. Easy to sow and grow.

* HALO — Bicolour pink, yellow, white, red.

* BLACK — Almost black single flowers.

HP ☀ ♦♦♦ ↕ 2m ↔ 60cm ⊙ Dec-Mar

Kiss Me Over The Garden Gate

Persicaria orientalis (syn. Polygonum orientale) — Is this the poster child of heirloom flowers? Reaching 2-3m tall in a single summer with its arching, pendulous dark flowers; it is eye catching and cherished by cottage gardeners and rare plant collectors.

TA ☀ ♦♦♦ ↕ 2m ↔ 50cm ⊙ Feb-Mar

Kiss Me Over The Garden Gate

Honesty

How Diggers membership preserves the best garden traditions

Heronswood and The Diggers Club have been gifted by the Blazey family to our recently established Diggers Garden and Environment Trust. Your membership and continuing support is vital to the preservation of these important properties.

It is but one of our Trust's historic garden properties which includes The Garden of St Erth, created by the Garnett family at Blackwood, as well as our 20 acre site at the foothills of Arthurs Seat where we are establishing a boutique botanic garden. This garden will house important plant collections of heirloom vegetables, flowers, fruits and rainforest trees.

We do want to show how important these plants are in the creation of our finest gardens and gardening traditions.

We have been busy upgrading our kitchen in Heronswood so that the exquisite architecture of our round room and dining room can be enjoyed by all Diggers Club members.

Edward La Trobe Bateman, the creator of the neo-gothic Heronswood building, was fresh from working on the Crystal Palace and part of the Pre-Raphaelite school that had such an influence on art in England 150 years ago. So this dining experience at Heronswood allows you to become part of its history; an experience that is unique in Australia.

Recently, anonymous benefactors have generously gifted their estate for the purposes of assisting our Trust's mission to educate gardeners and preserve our historic buildings, plants and important gardens.

We are emboldened to seek further support, whether it be your continuing membership, your encouragement of others to join us or for something more substantial, please email clive@diggers.com.au

Clive Blazey

Chair, Diggers Garden and Environment Trust

Introducing The Diggers Club

THE ACTIVIST GARDEN CLUB

Most gardeners know The Diggers Club through our preservation of heirloom seeds and our passionate opposition to genetically modified seeds. You may be surprised to know that Diggers bi-monthly magazine has become the No. 1 circulating garden magazine in Australia. We cover the issues that other magazines avoid because we can't be manipulated by advertisers.

Your membership funds our activities so we are free to shine the spotlight on multinational seed ownership of our food supply, deterioration of our soils and how gardeners can help alleviate climate change. Like the original Diggers who in 1649 opposed their landlord tyrants, we are an club of activist gardeners determined to lead sustainable lifestyles, bring our climate back into equilibrium and live in harmony with nature as we do in our gardens. We have more members than Australia's largest football club, more garden seeds and plant selections than any nursery and with our 7th book, more expert gardening advice and workshops than any other garden authority.

We cover the basics of how and when to raise seeds, select and grow plants, compost, prune and mulch as well. To enjoy our standard of gardening and be self sufficient in food takes no more than 5 hours a week - that's our club promise to show you how.

"There's no excuse for ugliness" when there are so many beautiful plants and gardens to choose from. It is what you exclude from your garden that creates its beauty, so visit our gardens and be inspired to create a garden that's anything but commonplace. Our members can visit four of Australia's finest gardens for inspiration!

Your Club dining room!

Exclusive dining for Diggers Club members inside the historic Heronswood House.

Free entry to 4 Gardens

Heronswood

Heronswood has the biggest collection of edible plants in Australia with a kitchen garden, vegetable parterre and herb garden, which are the source of the freshest food served in our restaurant. Club members can dine exclusively within the acclaimed historic building and experience life 150 years ago.

After lunch wander through the garden stimulated by beautiful perennial borders and seek advice. Our 1864 shop has a huge collection of heirloom seeds, fruit trees and perennials to take back home, and ask about our upcoming workshops.

St Erth

St Erth is a charming country garden just 60 minutes from Melbourne en-route to Ballarat, Daylesford or Kyneton. Set in the bush it has delightful displays of daffodils, an espaliered orchard, food forest and long lasting perennial border. The recently completed Garnett lecture centre is perfect for workshops and weddings.

Our team are there to answer your questions and supply your seeds, plants and books, and our café serves simple yet elegant food.

Both Heronswood and St Erth are Australia's first publicly opened gardens that are certified organic.

Cloudehill

Cloudehill is arguably Australia's finest cool climate garden. Set in the Dandenong ranges where most of our market flowers are grown, just an hour from Melbourne, amongst purple beeches, gigantic rhododendrons and magnolias are beautiful displays of wild flowers in spring, two magnificent herbaceous borders in summer and spectacular autumn colours through to winter.

Diggers members can purchase from a large plant nursery and a shop full of seeds, with rare and advanced plants for passionate gardeners and a comprehensive workshop programme for members.

Adelaide

The Adelaide Botanic Garden has the best collection of dry climate plants in Australia, set amongst the shadiest avenues of lush green evergreen trees it is a world class garden of great beauty. Enjoy the lotus pond, the rose garden, the world's rarest water lily and the incredible seed museum, all just 5 minutes from the city. The Diggers Garden Shop has the staff, plants, seeds and educational workshops to help you.

St Erth

Heronswood

Cloudehill

Adelaide Botanic Garden

Plant Selector index

Join The Diggers Club

CLUB MEMBERSHIP ☐ 1 year $49 ☐ 2 years $69

Mr/Mrs/Ms _____

Address _____

_____ Postcode _____

Email _____ Daytime phone _____

I enclose a ☐ cheque, ☐ money order or charge my ☐ Mastercard ☐ Visa

Card no. ☐☐☐☐ ☐☐☐☐ ☐☐☐☐ ☐☐☐☐ Expiry date ☐☐

Signature _____

NANEU

THE DIGGERS CLUB
PO Box 300
Dromana VIC 3936
Phone 03 5984 7900
www.diggers.com.au
info@diggers.com.au

Prices valid at time of printing and may be subject to change

Let The Diggers Club help you create a beautiful garden!